Corpus Christi

Padre Island and the Bay Area

By Vivienne Heines
Corporate profiles by Scott Williams and Vivienne Heines
Featuring the photography of Bryan Tumlinson

Photo by Bryan Tumlinson.

*Produced in partnership with
the Corpus Christi Chamber of Commerce*

Corpus Christi

Padre Island and the Bay Area

By Vivienne Heines
Corporate profiles by Scott Williams and Vivienne Heines
Featuring the photography of Bryan Tumlinson

Corpus Christi

Padre Island and the Bay Area

Produced in partnership with
the Corpus Christi Chamber of Commerce
Tom Niskala, Chief Executive Officer
1201 North Shoreline Blvd.
Corpus Christi, Texas

By Vivienne Heines
Corporate profiles by Scott Williams and Vivienne Heines
Featuring the photography of Bryan Tumlinson

Staff for *Corpus Christi, Padre Island, and the Bay Area*

Acquisitions: Henry S. Beers
Publisher's Sales Associate: Marlene Berg
Editor in Chief: Wendi L. Lewis
Managing Editor: Amy Newell
Profile Editor: Mary Catherine Richardson
Design Director: Scott Phillips
Designer: Matt Johnson
Photo Editors: Matt Johnson and Amy Newell
Contract Manager: Christi Stevens
National Sales Manager: Ronald P. Beers
Sales Assistant: Sandra Akers
Acquisitions Coordinator: Angela P. White
Proofreader: Allison L. Griffin
Accounting Services: Stephanie Perez
Print Production Manager: Jarrod Stiff
Pre-Press and Separations: Artcraft Graphic Productions

Community Communications, Inc.
Montgomery, Alabama

David M. Williamson, *Chief Executive Officer*
Ronald P. Beers, *President*
W. David Brown, *Chief Operating Officer*

© 2000 Community Communications, Inc.
All Rights Reserved
Published 2000
Printed in U.S.A.
First Edition
Library of Congress Catalog Number: 00-031479
ISBN: 1-58192-022-9

Every effort has been made to ensure the accuracy
of the information herein. However, the authors and
Community Communications are not responsible for any
errors or omissions that might have occurred.

Photo by Bryan Tumlinson.

Table of Contents

Foreword, 8
Preface, 10
Epilogue, 90

1 chapter one
Hustlers, Dreamers, & Visionaries, 14

For centuries, the Corpus Christi area has attracted settlers with its vast natural resources. Native Americans and Spanish explorers, smugglers and traders, ranchers and oil barons—all staked their fortunes on the Bay Area's shores.

2 chapter two
Tourism on the Bay, 22

The crescent coastline long ago earned the name "Texas Riviera," and a wealth of waterfront activities awaits visitors today. Tourists can stroll along the downtown seawall, set sail on the bay, explore culture at many museums, or experience underwater adventure at the Texas State Aquarium. Big-city fun with all the benefits of a coastal paradise—the Bay Area has it all.

3 chapter three
The Port's Economic Power, 32

The Port of Corpus Christi opened in 1926, and it quickly transformed a sleepy, small town into a thriving urban area. The Port has grown steadily throughout the years, and recent changes have further expanded its economic role. And with its new waterfront development, the Port now is offering a perfect blend of business and pleasure.

4 chapter four
Making a Home for the Military, 38

The region's three military installations provide key services to the entire nation and bring important benefits to the Bay Area, as well. Naval Air Station Corpus Christi, Naval Air Station Kingsville, and Naval Station Ingleside all serve to enhance economic prosperity and civic pride.

5 chapter five
The Pulse of the Region, 46

Quality medical care is never far in the Bay Area; more than a dozen hospitals and scores of clinics offer state-of-the-art services. This network of health-care providers helps residents maintain their physical well-being—and ensures their peace of mind.

6 chapter six
A Confluence of Cultures, 54

Throughout the Corpus Christi area, the arts and entertainment scene presents a world of possibilities to both residents and visitors. From symphony to sports, fun festivals to fine art, a variety of events keeps life lively year-round.

7 chapter seven
Bienvenidos to Business & Industry, 64

The Bay Area's economy continues to thrive, and even more prosperity is forecast for years ahead. The tourism industry is expanding, as are many businesses throughout the region. Also playing an important role are the Port of Corpus Christi and the area's three military bases. This eclectic mix creates a sure formula for future economic success.

8 chapter eight
Innovations in Education, 72

A solid educational system is a primary focus in the Bay Area; officials recognize that tomorrow's leaders must receive the best possible instruction today. From pre-school to post-graduate levels, academic institutions are preparing students to meet the challenges ahead.

PADRE ISLAND AND THE BAY AREA

Enterprise Index, 156
Bibliography, 157
Index, 158

9 chapter nine
Bounty from Nature, 80

Natural wonders abound in the Bay Area, and unspoiled scenery and abundant wildlife attract more visitors every year. Beaches and bays hold an array of environmental riches to be treasured and enjoyed.

10 chapter ten
Transportation, Communications, & Energy, 94

AEP-Central Power and Light, 96-97 • Port of Corpus Christi, 98-99 • Regional Transportation Authority, 100 • U.S. Cellular, 101
SOL Communications, 102 • Southwestern Bell, 103

11 chapter eleven
Manufacturing & Distribution, 104

Horton Automatics, 106 • Occidental Chemical Corporation, 107 • DuPont, 108

12 chapter twelve
Business & Finance, 110

Corpus Christi Chamber of Commerce, 112-113 • City of Corpus Christi, 114-115 • Hilb, Rogal and Hamilton Company, 116

13 chapter thirteen
The Professions, 118

Hunter & Handel P.C., 120-121 • Naismith Engineering, Inc., 122 • Collier, Johnson & Woods, P.C., 123 • Richter Architects, 124
Fields, Nemec & Co., P.C., 125

14 chapter fourteen
Real Estate, Development, & Construction, 126

Fulton Construction/Coastcon Corp., 128-129 • Moorhouse Construction Company, 130 • Wilkinson/Reed Development, Inc., 131
Prudential Real Estate Center, 132 • Haeber Roofing Company, 133

15 chapter fifteen
Health Care, 134

Driscoll Children's Hospital, 136-167 • Surgicare of Corpus Christi, 138 • Corpus Christi Medical Center, 139

16 chapter sixteen
The Marketplace, Hospitality, & Tourism, 140

Whataburger, Inc., 142-145 • Corpus Christi Convention & Visitors Bureau, 146-149 • Marina Grand Hotel, 150-151
Ramada Inn Bayfront, 152 • Pagan-Lewis Motors, Inc., 153 • Christy Estates Suites, 154

Photo by Bryan Tumlinson.
Next page: Photo by Bryan Tumlinson.

Foreword

The lifeblood of any community is its people, and the Corpus Christi Bay area is no exception. As we enter the new millennium, we look to the many people who have contributed their strength, talent, and vision to help make this area what it is today—a vibrant and fascinating place to live in and visit. In these profiles of local residents there exudes a dedication, discipline, and selflessness that makes their work and their lives notable achievements— and ones worthy of our recognition.

Dr. Hector P. Garcia, the late physician, civil rights leader, and patriot who died in 1996. "Dr. Hector" was awarded the Presidential Medal of Freedom by President Ronald Reagan in 1984. During Lyndon Johnson's administration, Garcia served in the U.S. delegation to the United Nations and is known as the founder of the American GI Forum, a civil rights organization born in Corpus Christi in 1948.

David and Elizabeth Chu Richter, a husband-and-wife team of architects and civic volunteers whose work has received national recognition. Their designs for urban bus shelters for the Regional Transportation Authority and a highway roadside rest stop for the Texas Department of Transportation earned awards from the American Institute of Architects, the U.S. Department of Transportation, and the National Endowment for the Arts.

Tony Amos, a British-born oceanographer and researcher at the University of Texas Marine Science Institute in Port Aransas whose work has fostered landmark anti-pollution legislation. His documenting of trash washed ashore helped create the international MARPOL treaty that bans dumping waste from ships at sea.

Luther Jones, Corpus Christi Mayor Emeritus (a formal, honorific title) and retired Army colonel whose post-political civic advocacy has included lobbying for the expansion of an upper-division, two-year school to a four-year university—Texas A&M University-Corpus Christi. A retired Army officer, Jones was unquestionably the city's most popular mayor— when he turned 80, friends and family feted him with a giant public birthday bash that drew more than 1,000 well-wishers.

Jesus Bautista Moroles, a world-renowned sculptor who was born in Corpus Christi and now lives in nearby Rockport. In 1982 he became the youngest artist and first sculptor ever to win an Award in the National Visual Arts Fellowship. His granite sculptures, characterized by their vigorous, clean lines, are displayed in many prestigious art museums and galleries nationwide.

Ernestine Bibbs, one of the founders of Bethune Day Care center, which serves underprivileged children. The nursery has been open for more than 50 years, providing care for the area's needy youngsters. Bibbs also was the first president of the local Young Women's Christian Association and is active in the National Association for the Advancement of Colored People.

Dick Messbarger, executive director of the Greater Kingsville Economic Development Council and a tireless promoter of the region's economic well-being. His persistence and widespread contacts were extremely valuable during the base-closure hearings, and his efforts helped to minimize military downsizing, particularly at Naval Air Station Kingsville.

Selena Quintanilla Perez, the Grammy-winning Tejano singer whose tragic 1995 death shocked fans around the world and trained the mainstream spotlight on Tejano music. Each year thousands travel to her hometown of Corpus Christi to visit a statue dedicated to the rising young star and to lay flowers at her grave. Selena was shot to death by the former president of her fan club on March 31, 1995.

Anne and Tobin Armstrong, longtime ranchers and visionary business leaders whose guest list reads like an international Who's Who. Anne, former U.S. ambassador to Great Britain, and her husband, Tobin, who manages a 50,000-acre ranch south of Sarita, Texas, have played host to visitors including former president George Bush, the Rockefellers, and Prince Charles.

Preface

My first visit to the Coastal Bend was years ago, during my college days in San Antonio. During spring break we stayed with friends who lived in Corpus Christi, and we also spent some time on the beaches at nearby Port Aransas. My most vivid recollection of the region was that it was lovely and very tropical, but especially that everything seemed particularly bright and light-filled. The area was drenched in an almost supernatural white light, shimmering in the intense south Texas sun.

A decade later, when my husband's job brought us to Corpus Christi, I remembered my first impression of the city. We crossed the Harbor Bridge and drove down the city's bayfront boulevard, Ocean Drive, and I was again entranced by the tropical brilliance of this gracious coastal community.

Since then, I have learned much about this area as I have traveled, researched, and written about it as both a reporter for the local newspaper and now as a freelance writer. It is a region known for its lustrous warmth, as well as its harsh climate and flat landscape. Its colorful history, its rich marine resources, and its diverse future combine to produce a landscape full of promise.

In writing this book, I have reacquainted myself with the Corpus Christi Bay Area's many assets and idiosyncrasies. It is my pleasure to share them with you.

Vivienne Heines

Photo by Bryan Tumlinson.

part one

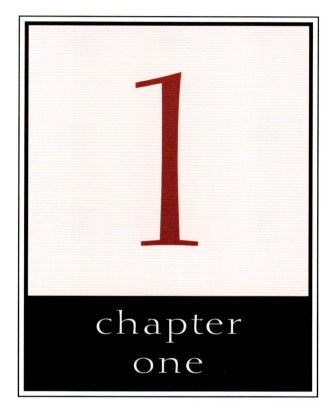

chapter one

Hustlers, Dreamers, &
Visionaries

Photo by Bryan Tumlinson.

Settlement of the Corpus Christi Bay area started with a colorful cast of characters who came, saw, and settled on this fertile and sun-drenched paradise—some motivated by idealism, many others by the lure of financial gain.

From pirates to ranchers, cowboys to oilmen, businessmen to developers—all were drawn to the region's priceless natural assets, including Corpus Christi Bay, vast available acreage, rich lands, and a wealth of natural oil and gas resources. Throughout the centuries, the most enterprising of these visionaries tried to parlay the crescent-shaped coastline and its natural assets into an attraction for others—an approach that still works its magic today on millions of visitors every year.

The first inhabitants of this coastal land were as fierce and distinctive as any of those settlers who came later—the Karankawa Indians. These Native Americans are best remembered for their gigantic stature and a penchant for cannibalism. The war-like Karankawa inhabited the Corpus Christi Bay Area and adjacent islands, living on fish, nuts, and the fruit of the cactus. They remained undisturbed until Europeans arrived in the early 16th century.

Photo by Bryan Tumlinson.

In 1519 Spanish explorer Alonso Alvarez de Pineda led a mission along the Gulf coast to chart unknown territory and to search for the rumored gold, silver, and other wealth that had inspired previous adventurers. De Pineda traveled the Gulf shore from Florida into Texas, exploring rivers, islands, and bays. Members of the expedition are believed to be the first white men to arrive at Corpus Christi Bay, and de Pineda reportedly chose its name because his discovery occurred on the Roman Catholic feast day of Corpus Christi.

Another Spanish explorer had a less tranquil visit to the region. Alvar Nunez Cabeza de Vaca, whose shipwreck landed him upon the Texas coast, was among a band of Spaniards enslaved by the Karankawa Indians. The Spanish prisoners remained with the Indians for six years, and many died during that time—some of them in Corpus Christi. De Vaca and three others finally escaped, and he later wrote about the land and its people. The accuracy of de Vaca's account has allowed historians to identify Corpus Christi as one of the sites in his story.

Soon other Europeans arrived, with many traders vying to establish themselves on the shoreline of the Gulf coast. Some set up ranches, others small trading posts, but everyone spent much time and energy defending homes and cattle from Indian raids. Spanish land grants were numerous, and the whole of Padre Island was granted to Nicolas Balli and his nephew, Juan, in the early 1800s. During this time, it is rumored that the famous pirate Jean Lafitte came to Corpus Christi Bay, and some say that he left a fortune in pirate gold and silver near Corpus Christi Pass. If so, his treasure remains hidden to this day.

Smugglers were among the next arrivals in the early 1820s, operating in small boats that trafficked in cotton, tobacco, and other goods headed illegally to Mexico. As more settlers came to the region, the opportunities for shipping contraband grew, and smugglers operated widely along the Bay Area.

In 1839 what is now the city of Corpus Christi was born, due largely to the efforts of Henry Lawrence Kinney, a young Chicago merchant with a magnetic personality and keen trading sense. Kinney's Ranch, a trading post he established on the bay shores, was intended to capitalize on the traffic in smuggled goods between Texas and Mexico. Kinney used his business acumen and considerable charm to negotiate with the Mexicans and the Texans, who both wanted to claim the property. Kinney also managed to repulse Indian tribes who periodically attacked the settlement.

In August 1845 General Zachary Taylor arrived at Corpus Christi and set up a camp for his troops, who reportedly had to slay 114 snakes around their campsite while clearing the land. Taylor, who was accompanied by Robert E. Lee, Jefferson Davis, and Ulysses S. Grant, established camp on the site of a future battle for land ownership between Texas and Mexico. When the troops left after a nine-month sojourn, the always-enterprising Kinney launched a campaign to lure settlers to the growing town, which he called the "Naples of the Gulf."

Local artist Dr. Sherman Coleman created the bronze statue *The Friendship Monument—Captain Blas Maria de la Garza Falcon*. The work was placed on Shoreline Boulevard in 1992. Photo by Bryan Tumlinson.

The Fulton Mansion, located in Fulton-Rockport, was built in 1877. The completely refurbished home is open for tours. Photo by Bryan Tumlinson.

Soon there were hotels, schools, and the other trappings of civilization, although the region remained a wilderness and Indian tribes continued to attack area settlers. One of the most significant of those early settlers was steamboat captain Richard King, who established the Santa Gertrudis Ranch about 40 miles southwest of Corpus Christi. This ranch later became one of the world's largest cattle domains—the King Ranch.

King, another charismatic and bold businessman, traveled to Mexico to recruit workers for his cattle ranch and persuaded an entire village to return with him to south Texas. In exchange for their labor, King promised to provide them with homes, food, and education—a considerable enticement for the impoverished villagers. Today, descendants of those *kinenos* (king's men) continue to live and work on the famous King Ranch, which comprises 825,000 acres of cattle land.

Kinney, the city's founder, died in 1861 during an ill-fated trip to Mexico. But his vision, including the beginnings of a deep-water port and vital links with Mexico, was complemented by the plans of other visionaries. In turn, they started rail and shipping lines, promoted the city's attractions, created the port, and enticed Navy leaders to construct a huge naval air station in the Corpus Christi area.

The Civil War left its mark on Corpus Christi, with Union blockades serving to nearly suffocate the commerce that had helped establish the city. But the Bay Area survived shelling by

By 1934, oil money brought a construction boom to Corpus Christi, and the city's skyline began to take shape. Photo courtesy of the Corpus Christi Museum, Doc McGregor Collection.

Federal warships, and once the war ended, a new era of prosperity began. This time, the region's fortunes hinged on the thriving cattle industry and the development of the hardy south Texas cowboy, inspired by the Mexican *vaqueros* who had long roamed the thorny south Texas wilderness.

Other forms of commerce also underwent major expansion at this time. The Corpus Christi Ship Channel Company formed in 1860, with the goal of dredging a deeper ship channel. City voters agreed to a $25,000 bond issue in 1871 to deepen the channel, greatly increasing the community's ability to participate in meaningful trade.

The area's fortunes pivoted on the discovery of natural gas in 1913 and of oil in 1930. Both events brought hundreds of workers, specialists, and merchants to the city. Also in 1930 the ship channel was deepened from 25 to 30 feet, and later to 45 feet. By 1938 Corpus Christi ranked fourth among the nation's ports in cotton shipments, and there were more than 7,500 producing wells in the port's territories.

It was in the 1940s that the military came to call Corpus Christi home. Drawn by the region's climate and proximity to water, Defense Department leaders decided to establish a naval air training facility on the bay front. There are now three Navy bases and an Army helicopter repair facility in the region, employing approximately 10,000 military and civilian personnel.

The collapse of oil prices during the 1980s forced the Bay Area to diversify its economy. The traditional economic base, which included the petrochemical industry, farming and ranching, and the military, was broadened to include tourism, service industries, broad-based manufacturing, and expanded health care.

Corpus Christi also is the birthplace of two major civil rights organizations, the League of United Latin American Citizens (LULAC) and the American GI Forum. Both remain active today.

Historically, the Corpus Christi Bay Area has always rebounded from setbacks caused by wars, epidemics, hurricanes, and fickle economics. The future looks bright as leaders of the modern Bay Area work to promote higher education at two universities that have merged with the Texas A&M University System. Other goals include maintaining and expanding the military presence despite base closures elsewhere and expanding port trade with Mexico.

Today the petrochemical industry still plays an important economic role, employing more than 10,000 workers at local oil refineries and chemical manufacturers. And 30,000 more are indirectly employed, adding to the industry's economic impact.

A statue located at Texas A&M University-Corpus Christi honors the late Dr. Hector P. Garcia, renowned for his work as a physician, civil rights leader, and patriot. Garcia founded the American GI Forum and was awarded the Presidential Medal of Freedom in 1984. Photo by Bryan Tumlinson.

As in the early days, tourism remains an integral part of the region's fortunes. During the 1980s, community leaders made great strides in augmenting the natural resources of sand and surf with major visitor attractions including the Texas State Aquarium, Lexington Museum on the Bay, and the Corpus Christi Greyhound Race Track.

The rich and fascinating story of the Bay Area continues. As Corpus Christi embarks on a new millennium, future chapters are sure to be as colorful and diverse as those in the past. ■

The Tule Lake Lift Bridge, which opened in 1959, connects to the Northside of the Port for rail and industrial traffic. Photo courtesy of the Corpus Christi Museum, Doc McGregor Collection.

Fans of fishing are lured year-round to the Corpus Christi area. With skill and a little luck, anglers can hook a variety of species, including speckled trout, flounder, catfish, amberjack, whiting, drum, pompano, red snapper, and Spanish mackerel. Photo by Bryan Tumlinson.

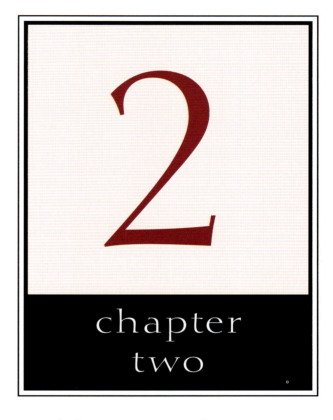

chapter two

Tourism on the Bay

The USS *Lexington*, decommissioned in 1991, now houses Lexington Museum on the Bay. During its service in World War II, the elusive aircraft carrier became known as the "Blue Ghost." Photo by Bryan Tumlinson.

In its early days the Bay Area became known as the "Texas Riviera." Even during the Great Depression, Corpus Christi's beaches attracted throngs of vacationers. Photo courtesy of the Corpus Christi Museum, Doc McGregor Collection.

From its inception, the Corpus Christi Bay Area's greatest strengths have been its location and natural assets. It sits inside the curved half-moon coastline of Corpus Christi Bay, which offers aesthetic beauty as well as a host of recreational opportunities for visitors. From fishing to kite flying, beachcombing to sunbathing, sailing to windsurfing, residents have always known how to enjoy the resources of this coastal paradise.

Trading on the bay traces back to the early days of the 16th century, when Spanish explorers first arrived at what they described as a "horseshoe-shaped" body of water. Explorers vied to claim the promising location for their own countries, while smugglers utilized the accessibility of the waterfront community for their own illicit benefit.

Early developers, who touted the region as the "Texas Riviera" and "Naples of the Gulf," lured settlers by promoting its location and beauty, as well as its proximity to the Gulf of Mexico.

Today's visitors are enticed by miles of beaches, abundant fishing and boating opportunities, and other water-based attractions. Situated midway between Houston and the Mexican border, Corpus Christi is the eighth-largest city in Texas. It boasts a sunny year-round tropical climate, with an average temperature of 72 degrees and 255 days a year of sunshine—attractive lures to sightseers, anglers, wind surfers, golfers, and nature lovers.

Corpus Christi is the second most-frequented visitor destination in Texas, with between five and six million visitors each year. Tourism is an economic mainstay, pumping more than half a billion dollars annually into the local economy.

Downtown Corpus Christi's main avenue is Shoreline Boulevard, a street that sets the tone of the community's water-based focus. This welcoming boulevard stretches leisurely along the sparkling blue waters of Corpus Christi Bay, flanked by hotels, restaurants, and office buildings.

For a relaxing stroll, there is no place better than the downtown seawall, a nearly two-mile long, 14-foot-high concrete stairway. Completed in 1941, it was designed by famed sculptor Gutzon Borghum, who also carved Mount Rushmore. Practical and pleasing to the eye, the seawall serves as a massive breakwater that protects downtown from the waters of Corpus Christi Bay.

The seawall's wide sidewalks also offer a prime place to jog, bicycle, roller-blade, or stroll and enjoy the cooling bay breezes. It is also a wonderful location for viewing activities on the bay, such as the Wednesday evening sailboat races. Visitors can see the statue of slain Tejano singer Selena and enjoy the shady retreat offered by eight Spanish-style *miradores del mar*. These gazebo-like scenic overlooks feature benches for sitting and have become popular sites for outdoor weddings.

Sightseers can find another serene spot at the Watergarden in the Bayfront Arts and Sciences Park. Here tired travelers can relax to the soothing sounds of a sunken fountain designed by New York landscape artist Robert Zion. Many museums are located nearby, including the South Texas Institute for the Arts, Corpus Christi Museum of Science and History, and the Asian Cultures Museum.

A little farther down the road is a neighborhood that offers a glimpse of Corpus Christi's history—Heritage Park. Here, nine old homes have been renovated and arranged to capture the city's past. The oldest of these homes was built in 1851.

Once past downtown, the bayfront's roadway turns into Ocean Drive—a seven-mile, scenic waterfront drive. Lined with stately homes and walking paths, Ocean Drive has been described as one of the state's most beautiful streets.

The view is enhanced by a series of waterfront parks, including the sprawling 43-acre Cole Park with its amphitheater, KidsPlace playground, and a handful of smaller parks farther south. These various attractions ensure that everyone can access the bay waters and share in the beauty of a coastal sunrise. Cole Park contains a fishing pier as well as an 18,000-square-foot model of a fortress. Summertime visitors can enjoy free concerts in the park, which are sponsored by the City of Corpus Christi. The concerts, which feature musical styles ranging from rock'n'roll to Big Band, are held Thursday and Sunday evenings.

The Harbor Bridge, Texas' second-tallest bridge, leads to Corpus Christi Beach. Here sit two of the city's most-visited attractions—the Texas State Aquarium and Lexington Museum on the Bay.

With dozens of live exhibits, the Texas State Aquarium has drawn more than three million visitors since it opened in July 1990. Aquarium residents include sharks, endangered sea turtles, manta rays, river otters, moray eels, and more—up to 250 species of sea life in more than 400,000 gallons of seawater. The building is designed to give visitors the sensation of descending gradually deeper and deeper into the Gulf waters. Among the most popular features are dive shows and "touch tanks." This hands-on exhibit gives youngsters and adults alike the opportunity to touch a shark's skin or let a hermit crab crawl on their palm.

A few blocks away is another hugely popular attraction, the decommissioned aircraft carrier USS *Lexington*, now known as Lexington Museum on the Bay. This legendary carrier, commissioned in 1943, served longer and set more records than any other aircraft carrier in U.S. Naval history. It was decommissioned in 1991 and arrived in Corpus Christi in 1992. Visitors can climb up the ship's many ladders, wander through the narrow passageways, and marvel at the vessel's history and size. Exhibits include vintage aircraft, models, and even a 16-passenger flight simulator.

Golfers will find scenic fairways at public, private, and semi-private courses throughout the Corpus Christi area. Photo by Bryan Tumlinson.

The bay provides a perfect playground for water sports, including sailing, surfing, and windsurfing. Photo by Bryan Tumlinson.

Known as the "Lady Lex" by sailors who served aboard her, she was the Navy's second Essex-class aircraft carrier. She joined the Navy's Fifth Fleet at Pearl Harbor and participated in almost every operation in the Pacific Theater during World War II. Her invincibility—despite the numerous attacks she endured—led to her being erroneously reported sunk four times by Japanese propagandist Tokyo Rose. And since the "Lady Lex" always survived, she became known as "The Blue Ghost."

Even more waterfront activities can be found in nearby Port Aransas, an island community that's popular with college students, families, surfers, and anglers. A free car ferry crosses the ship channel, and passengers enjoy watching dolphins frolicking in the surf. Known as the deep-sea fishing capital of Texas, Port Aransas draws anglers in search of king mackerel, red snapper, and pompano. This laid-back community also has lovely beaches, intriguing shops, and waterfront restaurants.

Area hotels and bed-and-breakfast inns offer a haven from the hectic world. Photo by Bryan Tumlinson.

Anyone who wants a break from the waterfront can head over to the Corpus Christi Greyhound Race Track, which opened in November 1990. This $21-million facility is owned principally by Southwest Florida Enterprises and its clubhouse features a full-service restaurant. The grandstand area has tables, a lounge, and theater-style seating as well as a food court. The track is completely air-conditioned, so visitors can enjoy pari-mutuel wagering in comfort year-round.

The Corpus Christi Bay area offers a wealth of activities for visitors and residents alike. Beyond the sandy beaches and glistening surf is a treasure trove of waterfront attractions, part of the city's continuing ability to trade on the beauty of the bay. ■

PADRE ISLAND AND THE BAY AREA

Fresh shrimp is always for sale at the Corpus Christi Marina, called the "T-Heads" by local residents. Photo by Bryan Tumlinson.

The boardwalk on Padre Island beckons visitors to embark on a relaxing beachside stroll. Photo by Bryan Tumlinson.

27

CORPUS CHRISTI

Above: Sightseers can discover a treasure trove of activities at the Texas State Aquarium and Lexington Museum on the Bay. Below: The Texas State Aquarium features dozens of exhibits that educate and fascinate. Photos by Bryan Tumlinson.

Visitors get a close-up view of an underwater world at the Texas State Aquarium. The aquarium complex contains 400,000 gallons of water and more than 3,000 animals. Photo by Bryan Tumlinson.

Corpus Christi's wind and waves provide a variety of recreational pursuits. The city is home to the annual U.S. Open Windsurfing Regatta. And every Wednesday, sailing enthusiasts can compete in a regatta on the bay. Photos by Bryan Tumlinson.

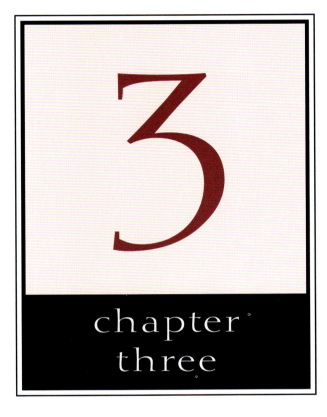

chapter three

The Port's Economic Power

The Port of Corpus Christi serves as a hub of international and national commerce. Photo by Bryan Tumlinson.

The Port of Corpus Christi has long been a significant transportation route and one of the region's most vital economic engines. With its vast sea networks and shipping capabilities, the port links south Texas to the rest of the world.

Creation of a deep-water port was a long-term goal of city planners. Community leaders and prominent business owners lobbied diligently for more than 75 years to obtain the federal government's designation of Corpus Christi as a deep-water port. That designation was received in 1922, when President Warren G. Harding signed a bill authorizing preliminary work on the project. In 1926 the Port opened for world commerce. This single achievement transformed Corpus Christi from a sleepy seaside village, largely dependent on agriculture and resort business, into one of Texas' major cities. As the port grew, oil was discovered and produced, heavy industry was attracted, and a huge naval air station was established.

Today the Port of Corpus Christi is ranked among the top 10 ports in the United States in terms of actual tonnage, and it plays a key role in the growth of Corpus Christi and the entire south Texas region. Economic benefits stemming from the port and related industries include 30,000 jobs, more than $1 billion in annual revenue, and approximately $66 million in taxes.

With a depth of 45 feet, the Port of Corpus Christi is one of the deepest ports located on the Gulf of Mexico. The port offers a full range of maritime facilities and services, from liquid bulk

The Port of Corpus Christi, which opened in 1926, brought an era of unprecedented growth to the Bay Area. Photo courtesy of the Corpus Christi Museum, Doc McGregor Collection. Top photo by Bryan Tumlinson.

docks and a bulk terminal to general cargo facilities capable of handling a variety of cargoes including automobiles and military equipment. The port also has acres and acres of additional land available for development.

Today, port leaders seek to continue building upon the economic foundation of the petrochemical industry by diversifying and developing new business opportunities for the citizens of south Texas. Over the years, the port has invested tens of millions of dollars to improve and build facilities aimed at attracting new business and cargoes. Diversification efforts have focused on military equipment, automobiles, project cargo, container shipping, cruise ships, and refrigerated cargo.

As the new millennium begins, diversification of the port has become a reality. In 2000 the port completed construction of a $10-million refrigerated warehouse distribution center for the import and export of refrigerated commodities from the United States, Mexico, and Central and South America. The refrigeration facility, approximately 100,000 square feet, is the most state-of-the-art on-dock refrigerated warehouse on the Gulf of Mexico. This project enables the port to expand globally as well as locally by providing new business opportunities for south Texans.

The port, in its pursuit of cruise ships, completed the first phase of an overall master plan that ultimately will create a waterfront development which will feature a mix of entertainment, cultural venues, and retail activities. The completion of phase one gives the port a facility that can accommodate cruise vessels as well as meetings, conferences, banquets, and other events. The facility, named the Congressman Solomon P. Ortiz International Center, opened in August 2000.

With this new facility, the port hopes to attract a cruise line to establish a home port in Corpus Christi. The port has been successful in attracting port-of-call visits, but ultimately it seeks to be the next Texas home port after Houston and Galveston.

Diversification of services remains the primary goal of port officials. This commitment to growth and strategy for success are perfectly reflected in the port's slogan—"The 21st Century Will Move Through Us." ■

The Port of Corpus Christi provides vital services to petrochemical companies and a host of other businesses. Photo by Bryan Tumlinson.

CORPUS CHRISTI

The Port offers a full range of maritime services and generates approximately $1 billion in annual revenue.

Above: The Port of Corpus Christi is among the nation's top 10 ports, and the Port continues to expand.

Below: A young visitor scopes out the ships from the Congressman Solomon P. Ortiz International Center. Photos by Bryan Tumlinson.

chapter four

Making a Home for the Military

Naval Air Station Kingsville is a top military facility for advanced pilot training. Photo by Bryan Tumlinson.

With 1,700 active-duty personnel, Naval Air Station Corpus Christi is the region's largest military installation. Photo by Bryan Tumlinson.

The arrival of General Zachary Taylor in July of 1845 set the stage for Corpus Christi's long and productive relationship with the military.

The city, known then as Kinney's Trading Post, had been founded less than a decade earlier. It remained small and relatively unknown until General Taylor's army set up camp on Corpus Christi Beach. Nearly 4,000 soldiers remained in the area for almost eight months, and they brought much attention to the small city. By the time General Taylor's troops had marched south to the Rio Grande Valley for the start of the Mexican-American War, the city had become quite well-known—a reputation that enhanced its ability to attract settlers.

Since then, the military's presence has continued to foster growth in the area. Examples include the Navy's decision to establish air training facilities during the 1940s and, more recently, to open a mine warfare headquarters in the 1990s. In addition, the world's largest Army helicopter repair facility is located in the Corpus Christi Bay Area. And ties to the military have been strengthened through the decades, even while other regions have lost military installations.

In January 1940 one of the area's major national projects was launched with the construction of Naval Air Station Corpus Christi. Navy officials had selected the station's site, nearly 12 miles south of the downtown section of the city, due to its isolated airspace, proximity to the water, access to cheap fuel, and for the mild, sunny climate that would allow pilots to train almost year-round.

Months before the attack on Pearl Harbor, the USS *Seawolf* SS-17 and USS *Aulick* 1 DD-258 docked in Corpus Christi. Photo courtesy of the Corpus Christi Museum, Doc McGregor Collection.

A war-ready Congress authorized the construction of 12 new military bases in 1940, the largest of which was the $100-million facility at Corpus Christi. The new naval air station was built on 2,000 acres near the city of Corpus Christi. Patterned after the Navy's air base in Pensacola, Florida, but on a larger scale, the base in Corpus Christi was completed in March 1941. It was dedicated in ceremonies that featured Texas Senator Lyndon B. Johnson and Navy Secretary Frank Knox.

Nine months later the Japanese bombed Pearl Harbor. The base produced 300 pilots a month, but that already-high training rate was doubled after the bombing. By 1942 the Corpus Christi base was the largest naval air training station in the world, and the only one to provide primary, basic, and advanced training. More than 35,000 aviators received their wings at Corpus Christi during the war, including former President George Bush. Half of all pilots who flew in the Pacific Theater during World War II were trained at Naval Air Station Corpus Christi.

The presence of the base also greatly contributed to the economic and cultural growth of Corpus Christi, giving rise to a vast array of restaurants, hotels, theaters, and other businesses catering to the military and their families.

The Navy has an equally strong presence in south Texas, with three bases in the Corpus Christi Bay Area. Naval Air Station Corpus Christi, the region's largest military installation, is where beginning students learn the basics of flying. Naval Air Station Kingsville trains advanced students to fly jets and conduct air-combat maneuvers, and Naval Station Ingleside is the Navy's headquarters for its mine warfare command. In addition, the world's largest helicopter repair facility, the Corpus Christi Army Depot, is housed at Naval Air Station Corpus Christi.

Aviation training is a major focus of operations at Naval Air Station Corpus Christi. The facility is one of three military bases in the Bay Area. Photos by Bryan Tumlinson.

Above: Naval Station Ingleside is headquarters for the Navy's mine warfare program. Tours of the facility are offered regularly. Below: The USS *Lexington* served longer and set more records than any aircraft carrier in U.S. history. The vessel was decommissioned in 1991 and arrived in Corpus Christi Bay the following year. Photos by Bryan Tumlinson.

However, the area's military missions were threatened during the Defense Base Closure and Realignment Commission hearings in 1991, 1993, and 1995. During the first round, Defense Department officials debated shutting down the Navy's proposed deep-water port at Ingleside. Local officials formed a military task force that vigorously battled to retain the remaining military facilities now housed in the Coastal Bend. Their evidence eventually convinced military officials that the Bay Area offers undisputed assets for the continued training of pilots, helicopter repair, and mine warfare consolidation.

Today the 4,400-acre Naval Air Station Corpus Christi employs approximately 1,700 active-duty personnel, 2,500 reservists, and 5,400 civilians. The military's labor force at Corpus Christi contributes approximately $333 million to the local economy.

The base's primary mission continues to be naval air training, with approximately 400 new aviators qualified annually. In addition, Naval Air Station Corpus Christi now houses a host of tenant commands. Among the tenants on board are the Commander of Naval Air Training (CNATRA), Training Air Wing Four, Commander Mine Warfare Group, Helicopter Mine Countermeasures Squadron 15, U.S. Coast Guard Group/Air Station, U.S. Customs, and the Naval Hospital.

One of the largest tenants is the Corpus Christi Army Depot, which developed when the Army took possession of a 15-acre tract at the base. The Army Aeronautical Depot Maintenance Center began operating on April 21, 1961, assigned with helicopter repair and maintenance for three engines and four airframes. By 1968 the facility was in full operation, providing repair and overhaul service to approximately 400 helicopters. In 1974 the name was changed to the Corpus Christi Army Depot.

As the largest industrial employer in south Texas, the depot has a huge impact on the area's economy. It employs approximately 3,000 workers with an annual payroll of $145 million.

The depot, known as CCAD, is now the largest facility of its type in the world. CCAD provides helicopter repair and overhaul capability to all U.S. military forces and to several foreign governments. It occupies facilities valued at $600 million on approximately 154 acres at Naval Air Station Corpus Christi.

The Corpus Christi Bay Area became home to yet another Navy facility during World War II. Commissioned on July 4, 1942, Naval Air Station Kingsville was originally intended to house four pilot squadrons, provide a base for fighter and bomber tactics, and serve as a gunnery school for combat air crew. In the latter part of 1942 the base also was home to a temporary basic training center for an overflow of Navy recruits from the Naval Training Center in Great Lakes, Illinois.

Training was sharply reduced following World War II, and the field was placed in a caretaker status in 1946. The land was leased to the University of Kingsville for use as an agricultural station.

The field was reopened as a naval auxiliary station in 1951, and it became an all-jet training base in 1960. In 1968 it was redesignated as an air station and now serves as one of two Navy bases that provide jet training. Top students from the Navy and Marine Corps come to Kingsville to learn to fly jets, drop bombs, fly formations, and perform air combat maneuvers. It is composed of two jet squadrons that produce about 170 Navy and Marine Corps tactical jet pilots annually. The pilots who graduate from Naval Air Station Kingsville go on to join U.S. carrier battle groups deployed around the world.

The station employs 2,000 people and has an annual payroll of about $45 million. The area's military presence was greatly enhanced in 1988, when ground was broken for Naval Station Ingleside. Originally intended as a homeport for the battleship USS *Wisconsin* and the carrier USS *Lexington*, the area was selected because of its quick access to the deep waters of the Gulf of Mexico, the well-protected waters inside the barrier island, the abundance of land, and the potential for expansion. In April 1991 the Navy changed plans for the facility, designating it the Navy's Mine Warfare Center of Excellence.

More than two dozen U.S. Navy ships are stationed at Ingleside. Photo by Bryan Tumlinson.

CORPUS CHRISTI

Above: Corpus Christi Army Depot, the world's largest helicopter repair facility, is located at Naval Air Station Corpus Christi.
Left: Hundreds of pilots receive training and flight qualifications each year at Naval Air Station Corpus Christi.
Opposite page: A crew conducts maintenance work on a vessel at Naval Station Ingleside. Photos by Bryan Tumlinson.

The impetus for developing the Mine Warfare Center of Excellence grew from post-Persian Gulf War analysis, which revealed that U.S. mine warfare forces needed to be revamped. Navy officials chose to consolidate assets and training in order to improve mine warfare capabilities. Support of the Navy's mine countermeasures fleet is now the primary mission of the station, which houses 25 ships, including the Navy's largest mine warfare vessel, USS *Inchon*. The base won the 1997 Installation Excellence Award and employs more than 3,300 military personnel and 350 Defense Department and contract civilians.

Military installations are important economic anchors to the region. Navy, Marine Corps, and Army personnel hold more than 15,000 jobs and represent a $400-million boost to the economy. Just as importantly, south Texans have welcomed the military with open arms and have fought to retain the military presence that has nurtured this area for more than half a century. ■

5
chapter five

The Pulse of the Region

HALO-Flight Inc. provides critically ill and injured patients with quick transportation to Corpus Christi hospitals. Photo by Bryan Tumlinson.

Health care is a $1-trillion business in south Texas and the Corpus Christi area plays a vital role in this growing industry. The Bay Area is a regional center for health-care services, helping residents from more than 30 south Texas counties.

Advances in cardiac care and cancer treatment, a partnership with the renowned M.D. Anderson Cancer Center in Houston, and an increase in assisted living facilities are keeping patients closer to home for specialized care. Today, about 24,000 people work in health-care services in the Bay Area, and the annual economic impact is nearly $900 million.

One of the earliest and most influential health-care providers in the Corpus Christi Bay Area was Dr. Arthur Spohn, who established the city's first hospital on North Beach in the early 1900s. In 1905 Dr. Spohn asked the Sisters of Charity of the Incarnate Word in San Antonio to come to Corpus Christi. The hospital that was formed as a result thrived briefly, then was destroyed by the hurricane of 1919. Today the doctor's name continues to be associated with health care in south Texas. The former Spohn Health System now is known as Christus Health—a group of local and regional hospitals that each includes the word Spohn in

Bay Area Medical Center, one of the area's newest hospitals, is located on South Padre Island Drive. Photo by Bryan Tumlinson.

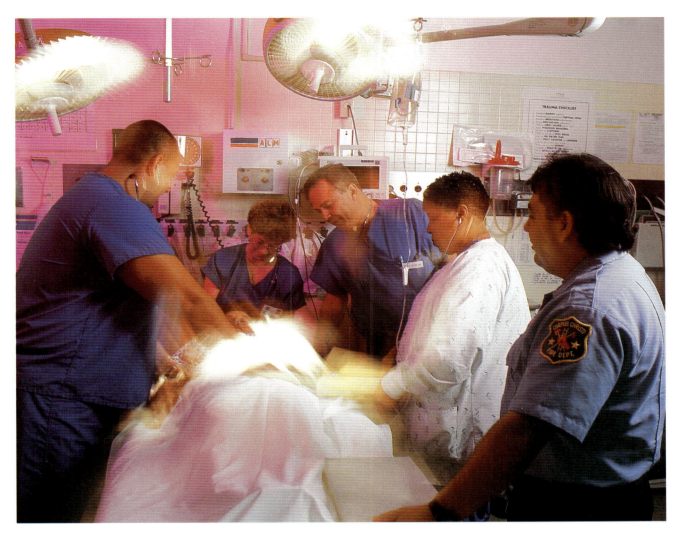

Spohn Memorial is one of six hospitals run by Christus Health in the Corpus Christi area. The facility operates one of the state's only Level III trauma centers. Photo by Bryan Tumlinson.

its name. Christus Spohn Health System is one of the largest and oldest health providers in the Corpus Christi Bay Area. In 1999 the former Spohn Health System merged with the system run by the Sisters of Charity of the Incarnate Word. This Houston-based system is a $3.4-billion Catholic conglomerate that ranks as one of the top 20 health systems in the nation.

Locally, the system comprises five area hospitals and collaborates with nine other providers, including hospitals and specialty clinics for occupational health and sports physical therapy. Specialized facilities include a new outpatient stem cell transplant program for cancer patients, which is run in partnership with M.D. Anderson Cancer Center in Houston, and a $24-million cardiac care pavilion that opened in 1998.

Among the Spohn hospitals are Christus Spohn Hospital Shoreline, the largest facility and foremost acute care medical center in the region; Christus Spohn Hospital South; Christus Spohn Hospital Memorial; Christus Spohn Hospital Kleberg; Christus Spohn Hospital Beeville; and Christus Spohn Hospital Alice.

The Columbia/HCA Healthcare system also provides a variety of medical facilities in the south Texas area, including five area hospitals offering comprehensive care. The Columbia/HCA facilities are Bay Area Medical Center, Corpus Christi Lab, Doctors Regional Medical Center, Northwest Regional Hospital, Surgicare of Corpus Christi, Corpus Christi Medical Center, and the Heart Hospital of South Texas. Columbia/HCA also operates North Bay Hospital in nearby Aransas Pass. Nearly 3,000 people work in this system, and it includes an $18-million Heart Hospital that opened in 1998.

Other facilities include the Corpus Christi Naval Hospital, a military hospital located at Naval Air Station Corpus Christi. This facility has served active-duty military personnel and retirees and their families since 1941. It serves approximately 120,000 outpatients annually, with a staff of 320 military and civilian personnel. It also supports branch medical clinics in Ingleside, Kingsville, and Fort Worth.

Driscoll Children's Hospital, located in the heart of Corpus Christi, is a nonprofit, acute-care teaching hospital. Opened in 1953 by the Robert Driscoll and Julia Driscoll and Robert Driscoll Jr. Foundation, it is a 188-bed private hospital that draws patients from more than 30 counties. The foundation was established in July 1945 in the will of Clara Driscoll, a south Texas businesswoman and philanthropist. Today, Driscoll Children's Hospital serves more than 85,000 patients annually with a staff of 1,200. It includes a neonatal intensive care unit and handles all aspects of health care for children.

Located next door is Driscoll Children's Rehabilitation Center, formerly the Ada Wilson Children's Center for Rehabilitation. The center, established in 1939, merged with Driscoll Children's Hospital in 1995. It is the only comprehensive rehabilitation facility in south Texas for children with disabilities. Patients range from those with suspected mild development delays to those with more severe and chronic handicapping conditions.

Horizon Specialty Hospital is a 31-bed, 150-employee facility that specializes in sub-acute medical care and comprehensive physical rehabilitation services. It focuses on assisting patients who are leaving the hospital and going to a more independent environment, such as home.

Corpus Christi Warm Springs Rehabilitation Hospital leases the entire eighth floor of Christus Spohn Memorial Center as a separate medical facility. This rehab center treats adults and children with brain or spinal injuries, stroke victims, and those with neurological or orthopedic conditions.

Volunteers in a variety of locally run programs bring cheer and comfort to hospital patients. Photo by Bryan Tumlinson.

More than 85,000 youngsters receive care every year at Driscoll Children's Hospital in Corpus Christi. Photo by Bryan Tumlinson.

A new and specialized cancer treatment program is offered by two local hospitals to serve patients who need stem cell transplants. Stem cell transplantation, used in conjunction with high-dose chemotherapy, is a treatment for certain types of aggressive cancers such as breast, ovarian, and testicular cancers, non-Hodgkin's lymphoma, and multiple myeloma Hodgkin's disease. The Corpus Christi Cancer Center first offered the program in November 1997, operating under the Columbia/HCA group. Spohn began offering the treatments in November 1999 after forming a partnership with the Houston-based University of Texas M.D. Anderson Cancer Center.

Rural medical service is aided by HALO-Flight Inc., an air ambulance service with a $2-million annual budget. It provides quick transportation to Corpus Christi medical facilities for critically ill and injured residents in a 16-county service area and 10 other counties. The total coverage area is approximately 61,000 square miles and serves a rural population of more than 729,000.

With a wide array of medical services, the Corpus Christi Bay Area's health-care facilities continue to expand. This constantly changing industry can anticipate a bright future as it keeps pace with technological developments and meets the needs of a growing population. ■

CORPUS CHRISTI

The Bay Area's newest residents get a warm welcome to the world at regionally acclaimed hospitals. Photo by Bryan Tumlinson.

PADRE ISLAND AND THE BAY AREA

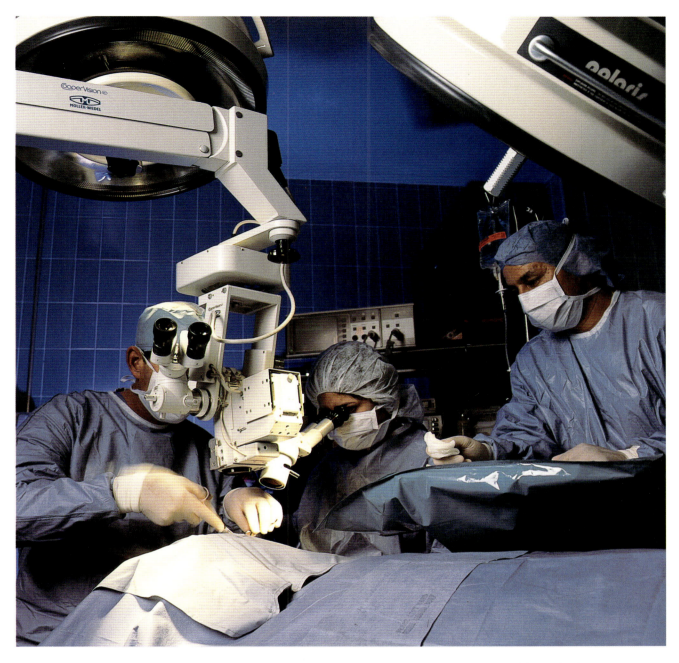

Bay Area Medical Center is one of five Columbia/HCA hospitals that provide residents with state-of-the-art care. Photo by Bryan Tumlinson.

6

chapter six

A Confluence of Cultures

Photo by Bryan Tumlinson.

In the Corpus Christi Bay Area, cultures converge, and the region reflects many backgrounds. This diverse population fosters a spirit of creativity, and the area enjoys many arts and entertainment options.

The death of Tejano superstar Selena in 1995 brought high-profile attention to the arts scene in Corpus Christi. But the vast wealth of culture in the Corpus Christi Bay Area goes beyond the memorable strains of Tejano music. It includes fine art, symphony, chamber music, jazz, rock—and the excitement of professional ice hockey and university football, baseball, and basketball games. In addition, festivals celebrating history and ethnic heritages contribute to the arts scene.

A cultural tour of the Corpus Christi Bay Area might begin with one of the most stunning buildings in the area, the South Texas Institute for the Arts. The institute overlooks Corpus Christi Bay from the barge dock in the Arts and Sciences Park. Designed by New York architects Philip Johnson and John Burgee, the museum emphasizes the art of the Americas, with special emphasis on Texas and the Southwest, and Mexico and Latin America. Currently, an extension is being designed by Mexican architect Ricardo Legorreta. Another venue included in the arts complex is the Antonio E. Garcia Arts Education Center, which offers programs in fine art and performing arts.

Another museum is the Asian Cultures Museum and Education Center, also located in the Arts and Sciences complex. Displays include thousands of Japanese Hakata dolls, as well as art and artifacts from China, Japan, India, the Philippines, Vietnam, and Indonesia. The museum also offers summer programs for children in calligraphy, origami, and Asian cooking.

Farther down Shoreline Drive to the south is the Art Center of Corpus Christi, which features exhibit space, studios, a gift shop, and a tearoom. The center specializes in promoting works by local and regional artists and is located on the median overlooking Corpus Christi Bay.

With three universities in the Bay Area, there is ample opportunity to see performances and fine arts exhibits at the campus studios and theaters. The arts buildings, galleries, and performance halls at Del Mar College, Texas A&M University-Corpus Christi, and Texas A&M University-Kingsville foster a tradition in fine arts and performing arts.

For a different kind of museum experience, there is the King Ranch Museum. Located about 50 miles from Corpus Christi in downtown Kingsville, the King Ranch Museum features exhibits such as saddlery from the ranch and from around the world, antique carriages, a custom hunting car, and vintage cars. An award-winning photographic essay by *Life* magazine photographer Toni Frissell, who spent five summers at the King Ranch documenting ranch and cowboy life, is also on display.

The arts enjoy a supportive community spirit in the Bay Area. The Art Center of Corpus Christi specializes in promoting works by regional and local artists. Photo by Bryan Tumlinson.

The Museum of Science and History takes visitors on a voyage to 1554 with its award-winning exhibit *Shipwreck*. Photo by Bryan Tumlinson.

Also in Kingsville is the 1909 Ragland Mercantile Building, which has been restored to its authentic architecture and now houses the King Ranch Saddle Shop. The King Ranch craftsmen not only make saddles, but also a variety of other leather products such as luggage and handbags. The building's award-winning restoration is listed on the National Register of Historic Places.

The John E. Conner Museum is located across the street from Texas A&M University-Kingsville. Among the displays in its ranching section are a chuck wagon and a typical turn-of-the-century ranch kitchen, including a hand-cranked washing machine. It also contains one of the state's largest collections of cattle brands and branding irons.

The performing arts scene is equally diverse, offering a wide range of theater and concert experiences. In the realm of dance, an exciting array of performers includes Ballet Nacional, a local folklorico dance troupe; Corpus Christi Ballet; and Corpus Christi Concert Ballet.

Broadway touring companies make their way to south Texas, presenting such hits as *Les Miserables*, *Fiddler on the Roof*, and *Stomp* at the Selena Auditorium in the Bayfront Plaza. The Harbor

Renowned architect Philip Johnson designed the striking, three-level Art Museum of South Texas. Photo by Bryan Tumlinson.

Above: The bay provides a scenic backdrop for a concert by the Corpus Christi Symphony Orchestra. Photo by Bryan Tumlinson.

Below: Bayfest, one of the area's largest annual festivals, draws thousands with food, fun, and top performers. Photo by Bryan Tumlinson.

Playhouse also presents a range of community theater offerings each year, including children's theater productions such as *The Wizard of Oz* and *Cinderella*. Musically, the menu is just as varied. The Cathedral Concert Series, an annual set of performances at the Corpus Christi Cathedral, has brought guest stars such as the Vienna Boys Choir, Brazilian guitarists, and a Russian chamber orchestra.

The Corpus Christi Chamber Music Society, the Corpus Christi Community Concert Series, the Distinguished Visitors in the Arts Series, and the Frederic Chopin Society offer impressive contributions to the musical scene. And those who prefer a more informal backdrop for their concerts can check out the annual Texas Jazz Festival or attend one of the summer community concerts held at the outdoor ampitheater in Cole Park, overlooking Corpus Christi Bay. A visiting Shakespeare troupe from Canada periodically gives performances on the outdoor stage. The Corpus Christi Literary Reading Series annually features nationally known authors presenting selections of their work; George Plimpton was the guest artist in fall of 1999.

Downtown Corpus Christi is also proving itself to be an up-and-coming venue for musicians and artists. There are a growing number of nightclubs and restaurants, as well as galleries for internationally renowned artists such as William Wilhelmi, whose work is part of the Renwick Gallery in the Smithsonian Complex, and Kent Ullberg, a sculptor whose statue of Jesus Christ is at the entrance of the First United Methodist Church on Shoreline Boulevard.

Local and regional festivals also offer a glimpse into the area's arts culture. Many such celebrations focus on the region's deeply rooted connection to the sea, including the Annual Deep Sea Roundup in Port Aransas, the Annual Shrimporee in Aransas Pass, the Bayfest in Corpus Christi, and the Harbor Lights Festival and Boat Parade at Christmas. Other popular events include the South Texas Ranching Heritage Festival in Kingsville, the Fulton Oysterfest in Fulton, and annual Greek and Czech festivals.

In the sports arena, the Corpus Christi Bay Area offers NCAA events at Texas A&M University-Kingsville. Rodeo fans will enjoy the Buccaneer Days PRCA Rodeo, held in the spring at the Memorial Coliseum in Corpus Christi. There's also the East West Powerboat Shootout, a national racing event held during the summer in Corpus Christi Bay; the Men's Pro Beach Volleyball Competition at Cole Park; and the U.S. Open Windsurfing Regatta at Oleander Point.

The city's professional hockey team, the Ice Rays, serves up its own version of excitement at Corpus Christi's Memorial Coliseum each October through April. A relative newcomer to the sports scene, ice hockey has taken the area by storm, and the home games are almost always sellouts.

With such an ebullient and far-ranging assortment, the Corpus Christi Bay Area's fine arts, entertainment, and performing arts are certain to satisfy even the most discerning visitor. The diverse array of cultural and creative offerings reflects the region's wealth of cultural traditions and artistic inspiration. ■

Kent Ullberg's statue of Jesus, entitled *It is I*, stands on Shoreline Boulevard. Photo by Bryan Tumlinson.

A pavilion and statue dedicated to Selena, the late Tejano singing star, is located in the bayfront Mirador del Flor. Photo by Bryan Tumlinson.

Tickets to see the Ice Rays are a hot commodity for sports fans; home games at Memorial Coliseum routinely sell out. Photo by Bryan Tumlinson.

PADRE ISLAND AND THE BAY AREA

Expert roping and riding comes to Corpus Christi every spring during Buccaneer Days PRCA Rodeo. Photo by Bryan Tumlinson.

Excitement lights up the nights during springtime's Buccaneer Days and at the bayfront Fourth of July festivities. Photos by Bryan Tumlinson.

PADRE ISLAND AND THE BAY AREA

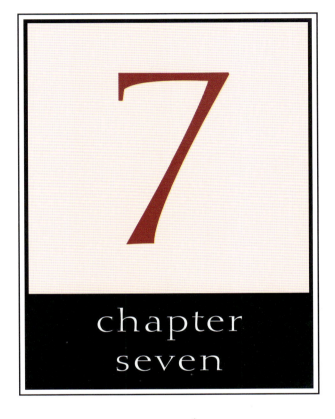

7
chapter seven

Bienvenidos to Business & Industry

Photo by Bryan Tumlinson.

CORPUS CHRISTI

Tourism continues to boom in the Bay Area and generates more than $550 million in annual revenue. Photo by Bryan Tumlinson.

In 1998 *Outlook* magazine named Corpus Christi a Choice City for Business—validating what area business leaders have long known about the welcoming economic climate of this thriving region.

The Corpus Christi Bay Area is expected to grow by 10 percent in the next 15 years. More residents, more jobs, and more new businesses are projected for the region.

Three organizations instrumental in shaping the economic growth and development of the Corpus Christi Bay Area are the Corpus Christi Chamber of Commerce, the Corpus Christi Convention & Visitors Bureau, and the Corpus Christi Regional Economic Development Corporation. All three organizations work with each other and with the local business community to position the area for increased growth in the 21st century.

The Corpus Christi Chamber of Commerce, which is the largest business organization in the Corpus Christi Bay Area, addresses local and state issues to enhance the business climate and foster business growth. The Chamber of Commerce provides leadership to link the business community on the local level and on national and international levels as well.

Tourism, one of the area's main industries, is supported through the dynamic efforts of the Corpus Christi Convention & Visitors Bureau. Recent marketing efforts have focused on attracting visitors from Mexico, Latin America, Canada, and Europe. In addition, the area has become a key location for conventions and meetings. The city of Corpus Christi is the state's second most popular visitor destination, after San Antonio.

Fostering new business relocations to the Bay Area is the role of the Corpus Christi Regional Economic Development Corporation. The corporation provides the necessary tools and research to actively seek out potential business, focusing particularly on high-tech industries and space-related corporations.

The low cost of living in Corpus Christi is a major factor in luring new businesses and people to the area. The cost of living in Corpus Christi is about 5 percent below the national average and on par with the overall Texas average. Real estate is abundant and affordable.

Employment opportunities are good, and there are many job training opportunities. The civilian labor force in the city of Corpus Christi tops 180,000, and the unemployment rate is about 6 percent. Projections for the area indicate that the strongest demand for workers will be in the fields of construction, the service sector, and durable goods manufacturing.

The petrochemical industry pumps more than $1 billion annually into the local economy and provides about 50,000 direct and indirect jobs. The industry accounts for more than 88 percent of the tonnage shipped through the Port of Corpus Christi. Products include plastics, pharmaceuticals, gasoline, fuel oil, solvents, asphalt, caustic soda, and parts for heavy equipment such as cranes and drilling rigs.

Adding to the economic mix are three military installations in the area that employ about 9,000 civilian and military personnel in aviation, ship maintenance, and other defense support.

Affordable real estate in and around Corpus Christi helps attract many new businesses. Photo by Bryan Tumlinson.

Other major growth industries in the Corpus Christi Bay Area include retail and commercial trade, teleservices, electronics, and manufacturing. The Texas State Comptroller's Office projects that the Corpus Christi and south Texas economy will grow faster than the state's economy. City leaders have launched a number of programs and incentives designed to foster business growth and expansion, including industrial districts, enterprise zones, and tax abatements.

New and expanded businesses include International Resistive Corp. Advanced Film Division, with more than 250 employees; First Data Corp., which is adding 200 employees to its existing workforce of 1,000; and Koch Refining Co., which opened a $40-million, centralized control center in late 1999. Koch employs 1,250 workers.

Additionally, Valero Refining Co. is expanding its heavy oil cracker, which breaks down oil into unleaded gasoline. Production has increased by 8 percent to 80,500 barrels annually. Valero employs nearly 500 workers. And Occidental Chemical Corp. is adding two co-generation plants to its Bay Area facilities.

Other petrochemical and manufacturing companies with Bay Area operations include Hoechst Celanese in Bishop, which employs more than 1,000 people; Hoechst Celanese Technical Center in Corpus Christi, with a workforce of nearly 400; CITGO Corpus Christi Refining, with 700 employees; and Coastal Refining & Marketing, Inc., with 360 employees.

Aker Gulf Marine Fabricators, Inc. has a workforce of 1,000, while E.I. DuPont de Nemours & Co. has more than 200 employees in Ingleside. At Coastal Javelina, Inc., Encycle/Texas is building a site for extracting recyclable nickel.

Agriculture has long been an economic mainstay of the region. Principal crops include cotton, corn, and sorghum. The Corpus Christi Bay Area is home to the world-famous King Ranch in Kingsville, the largest commercial ranch in the United States at 825,000 acres. The Santa Gertrudis cattle breed was developed on the ranch in the early 1900s, and in recent years the King Ranch has shifted its focus to agribusiness. Smaller ranches in the area produce Beefmaster and other breeds of cattle.

A relative newcomer to the economic mix are teleservices companies. These first came to the Bay Area in the early 1990s, attracted by the available workforce and digital communications infrastructure. Today, more than 3,200 personnel are employed in teleservices. Companies include First Data Corp., SITEL, APAC Teleservices, Billing Concepts, Millward Brown, and Futuremarket Telecenter, Inc.

Other major employers reflect the variety of businesses in the Bay Area. There is the HEB grocery chain, which employs 2,200 people; the Corpus Christi-based Whataburger, Inc. hamburger restaurants, with nearly 1,000 employees; Sam Kane Beef Processors, with 500 employees; Gulf King Seafood Co., with a workforce of 260; Horton Automatics, with 200 employees; and Wells Fargo Bank, with more than 200 workers.

The Corpus Christi Bay Area's economic outlook is bright as the 21st century begins. And with a thriving tourist industry, a welcoming climate for new and expanded businesses, a plentiful labor force, and the low cost of living, the area offers businesses a solid foundation for the future. ∎

Since oil was discovered in 1930, the petrochemical industry has played a key role in Corpus Christi's economy. Photo by Bryan Tumlinson.

PADRE ISLAND AND THE BAY AREA

Above: Oil companies provide jobs to more than 50,000 Bay Area residents.
Below: CITGO Corpus Christi is among the area's top employers. The company has new offices on Nueces Bay Boulevard. Photos by Bryan Tumlinson.

PADRE ISLAND AND THE BAY AREA

Ranching and farming, which brought prosperity during Corpus Christi's early days, remain economic mainstays in the region. Photos by Bryan Tumlinson.

chapter eight

Innovations in Education

Texas A&M University-Corpus Christi is located on picturesque Ward Island, only minutes from the downtown area. Photo by Bryan Tumlinson.

Students in the Bay Area attend public schools in 17 districts, including five in the city of Corpus Christi. Photo by Bryan Tumlinson.

Del Mar College, a two-year community college, offers occupational, academic, and continuing education programs. Photo by Bryan Tumlinson.

In the Corpus Christi Bay Area, officials place top priority on a strong educational system. And as the region attracts new residents, schools are meeting the challenge of educating more students.

Seventeen independent school districts serve the Bay Area, including five within the city of Corpus Christi. The public school districts outpace the state average on standardized tests, and students attend school in modern facilities.

A variety of cooperative programs with other institutions offers schoolchildren the opportunity for creative learning. Such programs include ventures with the South Texas Institute for the Arts, the Corpus Christi Museum of Science and History, the Asian Cultures Museum and Educational Center, the Corpus Christi Symphony, the Young Audiences programs, the Richard King High School Planetarium, the Texas State Aquarium, and the Junior League of Corpus Christi.

Additionally, the South Texas Public Broadcasting System, Inc., KEDT, produces educational programs with the Texas State Aquarium, Lexington Museum on the Bay, and the South Texas Institute for the Arts. These programs are broadcast nationwide.

The largest public school district in the Corpus Christi Bay Area is the Corpus Christi Independent School District, with 63 campuses and approximately 42,000 students in pre-kindergarten through grade 12. There are five high schools, 12 middle schools, 40 elementary schools, and six special campuses.

Public schools teach a state-adopted curriculum that sets stringent standards and follows the State Board of Education's 1993 initiative, "Raising Expectations to Meet Real-World Learning Needs." This program is designed to ensure that district graduates are prepared to begin a career or pursue higher education.

In the Corpus Christi Independent School District, the elementary schools include pre-kindergarten through 5th grade, middle schools include 6th through 8th grade, and the high schools are 9th through 12th grade. The schools use a dual approach of high expectations and strong academic standards. Teaching techniques include individualized instruction, media centers, laboratory methods, competency testing, computer-assisted instruction, team teaching, and diagnostic prescriptive techniques. Programs are available for at-risk, disabled, educationally disadvantaged, and gifted students.

The district also offers a summer remediation program for elementary students, summer school for secondary students, homebound instruction, adult and continuing education, a program for teen mothers, an alternative high school, and an alternative setting for students with disciplinary problems.

Public schools in the Bay Area follow a stringent, state-adopted curriculum, and computer instruction takes a high priority. Photo by Bryan Tumlinson.

Parents also can choose from a variety of parochial and private schools. The Catholic Diocese of Corpus Christi administers the largest group, with 26 parochial schools in a region that extends from the Corpus Christi area south to Laredo. Approximately 6,000 students attend these Catholic schools. Most other denominations also sponsor preschool and kindergarten programs, and some provide classes through middle or high school.

Del Mar College in Corpus Christi is a comprehensive, two-year community college considered one of the best in the nation. More than 16,000 students take credit courses, and another 12,000 are enrolled in non-credit courses at the college's two campuses. The college provides occupational, academic, and continuing education programs and has strong ties to business and industry in the Bay Area.

Founded in 1935, Del Mar offers one-year and two-year occupational programs designed to prepare students for immediate employment in business, industry or technical fields, or health-science careers. These specialized plans include legal professions, architectural drafting technology, auto body repair, and dental assisting. Del Mar's occupational graduates consistently score in the top of their fields on national and state licensing exams.

Dr. Hector P. Garcia Plaza, on the campus of Texas A&M-Corpus Christi, was built in honor of the noted physician and human-rights activist. Photo by Bryan Tumlinson.

Del Mar also offers two-year academic degrees in more than 50 major disciplines such as English, pre-medicine, marketing, and studio art. Many students receive two years of bachelor's degree instruction at Del Mar, then attend other accredited colleges and universities.

The college also maintains a strong cultural presence, hosting more than 100 music concerts, teleconferences, and workshops in the community each year. Most of the events are provided at little or no charge.

Other institutions of higher education include Texas A&M University-Corpus Christi, with a student enrollment of more than 5,800. The university expanded in 1994 from an upper-level school to a four-year, comprehensive university, adding 1,000 students a year and hiring new faculty. Today, Texas A&M-Corpus Christi boasts a student-faculty ratio of 16:1. An aggressive building campaign has resulted in more than $100 million in new construction on the "island campus" since 1990.

In 1998 and 1999 annual college guides, *U.S. News & World Report* ranked Texas A&M-Corpus Christi as the top public regional university in Texas. The poll divides the country's schools into national and regional categories, and then ranks them based on such factors as academic reputation, SAT/ACT scores, acceptance rate of applicants, the high school standing of college freshmen, faculty, financial resources, and student retention.

Texas A&M-Corpus Christi offers 56 degree programs in four academic colleges: Arts and Humanities, Business, Education, and Science and Technology. Among its best-known programs is nursing. Texas A&M University-Corpus Christi was the first university in Texas to be accredited by the National League for Nursing for its Registered Nurse-Bachelor of Science in Nursing program. The university also offers a Master of Science in Nursing.

Teacher certification, another popular offering, is available in a variety of fields. There also are pre-professional programs including pre-dental, pre-law, pre-medical, pre-optometry, and pre-veterinary medicine. And the Early Childhood Center at Texas A&M-Corpus Christi is a laboratory school with state-of-the-art, bilingual instruction in English and Spanish, and other innovations in early-childhood learning.

Graduate studies in mariculture and environmental science take advantage of the area's island location and proximity to the bay. The university is home to the Center for Coastal Studies, the Center for Bioacoustics, and the National Spill Control School.

Texas A&M University-Kingsville is a diverse and comprehensive university located about 50 miles south of Corpus Christi in the historic town of Kingsville. Founded in 1925, it enrolls approximately 6,000, including students from more than 50 nations.

Known as one of the state's most affordable universities, Texas A&M-Kingsville boasts nationally recognized programs in engineering, the sciences, and agriculture. Specialized facilities include the Citrus Center in the Rio Grande Valley town of Weslaco, where the sweet grapefruit known as the Ruby Red was developed.

At Texas A&M-Kingsville, students can receive bachelor's degrees in more than 65 fields, and master's degrees in 38 major fields. Newly established degree programs include criminology anthropology, gerontology, and English as a second language.

The vast and varied educational opportunities in the Corpus Christi Bay Area represent the community's commitment to its young people through academics, innovation, technology, and research. With an eye firmly to the future, the area's educators are employing the best resources available to help students achieve their academic goals. ■

Children in preschool through third grade receive instruction at the Early Childhood Development Center, located at Texas A&M-Corpus Christi. Photos by Bryan Tumlinson

A statue on the campus of Texas A&M University-Kingsville features the school mascot, the javelina. Photo by Bryan Tumlinson.

More than 6,000 students attend Texas A&M-Corpus Christi. The school offers study in more than 50 degree programs. Photos by Bryan Tumlinson.

9
chapter nine

Bounty From Nature

Photo by Bryan Tumlinson

The Corpus Christi Bay Area has truly been blessed with natural beauty. Its abundance of coastal scenery and warm climate have consistently attracted tourists from all walks of life. Now, a new group of tourists—those with an eye for ecology—are discovering the Bay Area.

More and more visitors come here specifically to enjoy the environmental treasures, including thousands of migratory birds that travel through the area along a route called the Central Flyway. Bird watchers have long known that this region serves as a spring stopover for trans-Gulf migrants heading north. At certain times, the fields, bushes, and trees are literally filled with tanagers, orioles, flycatchers, vireos, thrushes, and warblers.

Texas is a mecca for birders, with more than 600 species—one of the most diverse bird populations in North America. And the Gulf coast is particularly diverse, containing more than 75 percent of the state's species. State and local leaders, recognizing the immense potential of the state's birding attractions, have in recent years established the Great Texas Coastal Birding Trail—a 500-mile tour of parks, lands, refuges, ranches, and beaches—to guide birders to the state's abundant avian resources. In the Corpus Christi Bay Area alone, more than 50 sites are listed for premier bird watching.

Whether on land or by water, prime fishing spots are always easy to find throughout the Bay Area. Photo by Bryan Tumlinson.

Goose Island State Park is home to the Lamar Oak, the largest coastal live oak in Texas. Photo by Bryan Tumlinson.

The region now is known as one of birding's "hot spots," especially in spring and fall. Within a three-hour drive from Corpus Christi are four national wildlife refuges; a national seashore; five National Audubon Society sanctuaries; the privately operated Welder Wildlife Foundation's Refuge; numerous state, county, and city parks; and a variety of ranchlands. With little effort, any visitor can witness a great blue heron searching for its dinner in the coastal marshland or spy an iridescent painted bunting in the bushes.

One of the area's most beautiful natural wonders is Padre Island National Seashore, the world's longest barrier island. It stretches for 113 miles along the Texas coast, from Corpus Christi nearly to Mexico, and is one of the last barrier islands that remains mostly undeveloped.

Once home to the fierce Karankawa tribe, Padre Island was named to honor a missionary who worked among the natives more than a century ago. Today the island is linked to the mainland by the J.F.K. Causeway. The north end of the island consists of hotels and condominiums, a country club, restaurants, and stores. But most of the island—80 miles—is encompassed by Padre Island National Seashore, a secluded haven for anglers, surfers, beachcombers, and campers. Visitors can enter the national seashore through Malaquite Beach, where there is a visitor center with information, exhibits, a small store, free public showers, and paved parking.

Padre Island National Seashore is the largest undeveloped barrier island in the continental United States. The park is open to visitors year-round. Photo by Bryan Tumlinson.

Nearby is Port Aransas, a fishing village that has long lured anglers from all over the country. It was a favorite vacation destination of President Franklin Delano Roosevelt, and one of the town's older restaurants still displays a tarpon fish scale bearing FDR's signature.

Port Aransas is located at the northern tip of Mustang Island, one of the barrier islands along the central Texas coast. Mustang Island was named for the wild horses that once roamed its 18-mile-long beach. Early residents of this rustic village made their living by fishing and catching sea turtles—some as immense as 500 pounds. Today's economy relies on both fishing and tourism, and Port Aransas is especially popular with college students during the spring break season.

To reach Port Aransas from Harbor Island in Aransas Pass, visitors can take a free, five-minute ferry ride across the Corpus Christi Ship Channel. The ferry operates every day of the year, and the trip provides an opportunity to see dolphin, brown and white pelicans, and other birds.

This is another town that knows how to welcome its feathered friends. Bird watchers will want to visit the Port Aransas Birding Center, as well as four designated sites on the Great Texas Birding Trail. In addition to providing a habitat for year-round and migrating species, the Center's wetlands park also contains vegetation areas designed to lure the tiny, colorful hummingbirds that arrive each spring. In Port Aransas, these fascinating little birds even are honored with an annual festival.

Another bird-watching event for this area is the arrival of the rare whooping cranes that migrate to the nearby Aransas National Wildlife Refuge from Canada each winter. This flock is the world's only one that breeds in the wild, and it contains more than 150 of these beautiful, endangered birds. The comeback of the whooping crane is a story in itself. Numbers have rebounded from only 22 birds a half-century ago to more than 330 today, thanks to massive efforts to save the species. Whooping crane researchers and fans often visit during the winter, when they can take tour boats into the refuge to watch the flock.

Farther to the south is Baffin Bay, known for its trophy trout. Located about 20 miles south of Kingsville and 70 miles south of Corpus Christi, Baffin Bay has earned a reputation as a great place to relax and fish. This quiet community attracts serious anglers, who face an additional challenge from tricky rock formations just below the water's surface.

Surf and sand provide a perfect pathway for an afternoon outing on horseback. Photo by Bryan Tumlinson.

By kayak, boaters can enjoy a close-up view of the Bay's beauty. Photo by Bryan Tumlinson.

The historic town of Kingsville, in an area once known as the Wild Horse Desert, is another destination with many natural assets. Founded in 1904, Kingsville occupies land that was once part of the Rincon de Santa Gertrudis Mexican Land Grant. The land was purchased in 1835 by steamboat Captain Richard King. He established a cow camp on Santa Gertrudis Creek and began one of the world's most celebrated ranching legacies. But when King first started out, the area was so sparsely populated that he had to go to Mexico to hire workers.

Today, the 825,000-acre King Ranch, a National Historic Landmark, is recognized as the birthplace of the American ranching industry. Covering more than 1,300 square miles, it is larger than the entire state of Rhode Island. Yet it has shrunk from its maximum size; at one time, King Ranch holdings included close to 10 million acres in seven counties. In addition to cattle, the ranch also has produced several Kentucky Derby winners including Assault, who won the Triple Crown in 1946.

Tours of the ranch are conducted daily, and visitors also can take nature or birding tours to view the diverse wildlife on the ranch. A wide variety of tropical and migratory birds can be found here, as well as white-tailed deer, javelinas, and coyotes.

With such an abundance of natural assets, it's no wonder that the Corpus Christi Bay Area has become such a popular destination for those who love the outdoors. In the Bay Area, the opportunities to enjoy nature are boundless. ■

Photo by Bryan Tumlinson.

CORPUS CHRISTI

Bird-watching is a popular pastime for residents and visitors alike. The Bay Area's abundant natural resources make it a haven for hundreds of species of birds. Photos by Bryan Tumlinson.

Epilogue

At the turn of the last century, the Corpus Christi Bay Area was a sleepy but promising town, lined with unpaved streets where farmers, ranchers, traders, and resident visionaries mingled. The 20th century brought unimaginable changes and challenges to the port area; fortunes rose with agriculture and cattle ranching, then later with the discovery of oil and gas. Meanwhile the increasing popularity of tourism created a resort community, and the region began to assume the character that it retains today—environmentally unique, demographically diverse, rich with opportunity, and ever-welcoming to newcomers and visitors alike.

Today, as the Bay Area enters the new millennium, its prospects have never been brighter. Corpus Christi is one of the state's top travel destinations, and the area features a multitude of natural and man-made attractions. Beaches and bays offer inviting sites for swimming, fishing, and water sports. In addition, the area's unspoiled environment is a haven for nature lovers to experience the great outdoors. Museums, festivals, and cultural attractions also make the region enticing to thousands of visitors annually.

Residents enjoy a hospitable climate, thriving business scene, rapidly growing university system, and burgeoning opportunities that make the Bay Area a good place to live and work. And new businesses continue to locate in and around Corpus Christi, drawn by steady economic growth, quality health care and education, and excellent transportation systems, including a deep-water port.

The outlook is promising for a dynamic future in this sparkling city by the sea. With its unparalleled natural resources and waterfront location, this region remains positioned to continue its development as one of the Gulf Coast's most enticing destinations.

Photo by Bryan Tumlinson.

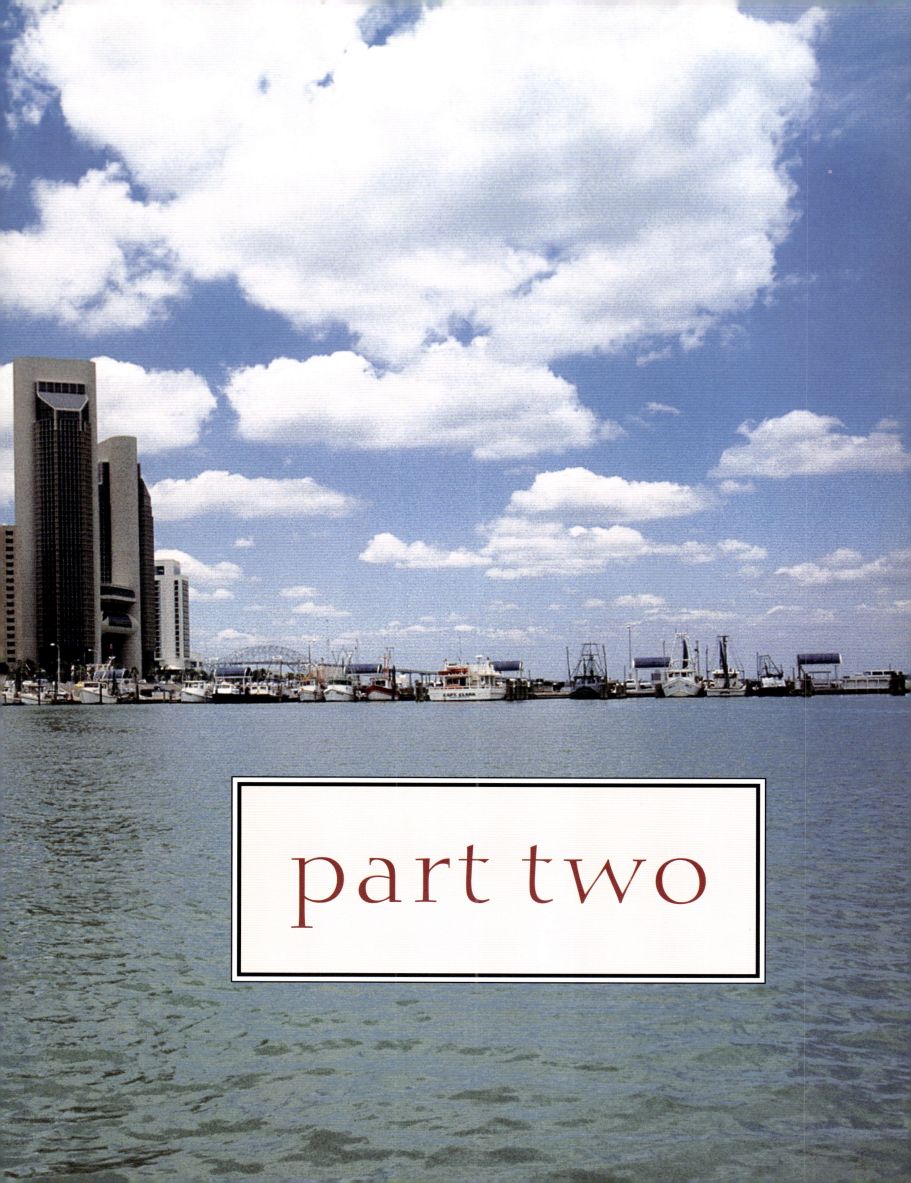
part two

10
chapter ten

Transportation, Communications, & Energy

AEP-Central Power and Light, 96-97
Port of Corpus Christi, 98-99
Regional Transportation Authority, 100
U.S. Cellular, 101
SOL Communications, 102
Southwestern Bell, 103

Photo by Bryan Tumlinson.
Photo on pages 92-93 by Bryan Tumlinson.

AEP-Central Power and Light

Many things have changed in the world of electricity since Central Power and Light Co. first began providing power to South Texans in 1916, but the company's commitment to serve the customer has remained the same.

AEP-CPL service crews cover a 44-county area of South Texas, serving over 627,900 customers.

The most notable change for CPL is the 2000 merger between its former parent company, Central and South West Corp., and American Electric Power, based in Columbus, Ohio.

The new AEP-CPL is ready to meet opportunities and challenges of the future as it remains dedicated to offering reliable, low-cost energy with nationally recognized customer service. Over the last two years, AEP has ranked among the top five electric companies in customer satisfaction, according to the American Customer Satisfaction Index.

Based in Corpus Christi, AEP-CPL supplies electric service to more than 627,900 customers in a 44,000-square mile area. It is part of the AEP family, which serves more than 4.8 million domestic customers in 11 Midwestern and mid-Atlantic states—and approximately 4 million customers outside the U.S. through direct holdings and joint ventures.

AEP operates more than 186,000 miles of overhead and underground distribution lines—enough to reach the moon. The company's 11-state distribution territory covers 197,000 square miles, comprising eight operating regions.

That's a far cry from its early days, when the former CPL delivered ice as well as electricity, and ran the streetcars in Laredo. Its origins began in 1914, with two St. Louis, Missouri, entrepreneurs named Ralph W. Morrison and Warner S. McCall, who bought the electric, gas, water, and street railway franchise in Laredo. Later, they purchased additional utilities and incorporated their company under the name of Central Power and Light on November 2, 1916. The early years were lean as the two businessmen built an empire in the region nicknamed "the cactus patch." CPL was sold to Middle West Utilities in 1925.

The stock market crash in 1929 was largely responsible for the 1932 bankruptcy of Middle West Utilities, although CPL continued its service uninterrupted. During World War II, CPL meter readers rode bicycles to conserve gas and women increasingly joined the company's work force.

Following the war, the company's growth was enormous, with a tripling of electrical demand between 1946 and 1955.

All-electric living was the style in the 1960s, and CPL extolled the virtues of the Gold Medallion Home. But the national energy crisis of the 1970s caused CPL's fuel expenses to skyrocket. As the result of natural gas shortages and federal legislation, CPL began to diversify its fuel sources. The coal-fired Coleto Creek Power Station came on line in 1980 and the South Texas Project Electric Generating Station became the state's first operational nuclear plant in 1988.

Patsy Torres, with the AEP-CPL Positive Force Tour, brings a dynamic stay-in-school message to South Texas school children.

PADRE ISLAND AND THE BAY AREA

In the 1990s, the company focused its attention on the future, renewing its commitment to understanding and meeting customer needs. Besides providing reliable electricity at competitive prices, the company and its employees contribute significantly to improving the quality of life in the communities they serve. The company's community relations efforts include fund-raising campaigns and educational programs. Support for education includes specialized energy workshops for teachers, school-business partnerships, and "Watts on Wheels," an energy education program that travels to schools.

AEP-CPL's goal is to satisfy customers from their first contact with the company—whether it's a request for power at a construction site, the start-up of service to a residence, or responding to a call reporting lights out. AEP-CPL's call center provides customers with telephone access 24 hours a day, seven days a week. Customers can make all their requests by calling a toll-free telephone number.

Partnerships with the community, always an important part of AEP-CPL's business presence, continue to reflect the company's commitment to its communities. AEP-CPL's economic development initiatives help existing businesses become more competitive, while working to draw new businesses to the region.

A commitment to environmental stewardship drives the dedication of AEP-CPL employees to go "beyond compliance"

The AEP-CPL Customer Service Center handles customer calls and inquiries 7 days a week, 24-hours a day.

and to strive for leadership in establishing environmentally and scientifically sound practices and benchmarks.

AEP stands today as an exciting, energetic company, with diverse resources and enormous opportunities for their application. As restructuring of the electric utility industry gives life to a vital energy market and new technologies meet the vastly divergent energy needs of the future, AEP will continue to emerge as a 21st Century energy leader for its customers, shareholders, and employees. ■

The AEP-CPL transmission grid delivers reliable electric service to a 44,000-square mile area in South Texas from Rocksprings down the Rio Grande to Brownsville and back up the Gulf of Mexico to Bay City.

Port of Corpus Christi

The Port of Corpus Christi has long been the economic engine that drives South Texas, and its strategic location and superb facilities position it to become a significant player in global trade well into the 21st century.

The nation's fifth largest port is located midway along the Texas coast on the Gulf of Mexico with close access to Mexico, Houston, San Antonio, and the Rio Grande Valley. Its modern multi-purpose facilities are ideal for a variety of cargoes, while the region's warm, arid climate provides the perfect setting for year-round operations.

Customers benefit from the Port's 45-foot channel depth (and headed toward 50 feet), more than 125 acres of open storage and fabrication sites, heavy lift capabilities, quick access to the Gulf of Mexico, dockside rail from multiple carriers, excellent highway access, a flexible and productive labor force, and approximately 338,500 square feet of covered dockside storage. In addition, the Port of Corpus Christi Foreign Trade Zone No. 122 streamlines U.S. Customs paperwork, allowing companies to reduce, defer, or avoid duties on imports.

The Port of Corpus Christi and the Port Industries situated along the Corpus Christi Ship Channel and nearby La Quinta Ship Channel generate 9,000 direct and 31,000 indirect high-wage jobs with a combined payroll of more than $1 billion.

The Port serves as the hub for the region's petrochemical industry with several refineries and chemical plants situated along its two channels. Chemical plants supply base commodities for industries throughout the world, while the refineries handle 5 percent of the nation's refining capacity.

Meanwhile, the Port's commitment to protecting and preserving the environment allows residents to enjoy air and water that are among the cleanest of any industrial-based city in the United States, and positions the Port for additional expansion at Port and Port Industries facilities.

French Naval Ship, one of many foreign ships the port greets throughout the year.

With the basic components in place, the Port of Corpus Christi is looking for ways to diversify, with several projects already in the works designed to increase business and create more high-wage jobs. The Port prefers to seek private investment to help fund its port-related activities and shies away from using public tax money.

Additions and improvements to Port facilities include:
• Refrigerated Warehouse Distribution Center: The Port of Corpus Christi and Berkshire Cold Storage have joined forces to build a state-of-the-art, 99,520-square-foot, refrigerated warehouse to serve the export/import markets of North America, Mexico, Central and South America, Europe, and Africa.
• The Waterfront Development Project: The first phase of this project features a cruise ship terminal, conference center, banquet exhibition area, and restaurant. This state-of-the-art facility is designed to provide a wide range of amenities for all types of corporate meetings, training seminars, and social functions. It's located on the Corpus Christi Ship Channel within walking distance of many tourist and civic attractions, and less than a mile from Corpus Christi's downtown business and social district.

The conference center is designed to provide visitors with majestic views of the channel and harbor, a professional staff, exceptional service, delicious cuisine, comfortable, flexible

The port and its employees take part in the local 4th of July celebration, 1999.

meeting areas, full-spectrum lighting, ergonomic seating, and millennium-age audio/visual presentation equipment. The port eventually plans to add entertainment and retail activities to the area.

• Joe Fulton International Trade Corridor: This 11.5-mile rail-and-road project will significantly improve access to more than 2,000 acres of land along the north side of the channel for existing and future development. It also will make available some 1,200 acres for real estate development as marine terminals and industrial sites. The fully funded project will connect two major highway components, establish efficient links between highway, marine, and rail transportation, enhance access to existing industries, and facilitate international trade. This NAFTA-designated highway will be a cornerstone of trade with Mexico in the 21st century.

• Channel Improvement Project: Work is under way to deepen the Corpus Christi Ship Channel from 45 feet to 50 feet to accommodate larger vessels, increase shipping efficiency, and enhance navigation safety. The Port of Corpus Christi and the U.S. Corps of Engineers also are evaluating widening the channel across Corpus Christi Bay from 400 feet to 500 feet and extending La Quinta Channel to provide deepwater access to more than 900 acres of waterfront property.

• La Quinta Trade Gateway: This state-of-the-art container shipping facility along the north shore of Corpus Christi Bay is designed to capitalize on the growing container business in the Gulf of Mexico, which is projected to grow at an annual rate of six percent until 2010. This deepwater site has close access to highways and rail. More than 700 acres of this 1,100-acre project

The port works closely with the military on the deployment of military equipment and supplies.

have been identified for commercial real estate development related to container trade, such as trucking, distribution, and support services. As part of this project, the Port of Corpus Christi will build a satellite operation in San Antonio to distribute containers unloaded in Corpus Christi and shipped to San Antonio.

• Harbor Island: The Port of Corpus Christi is determining the "best use" for this 300-acre site on the Gulf of Mexico. Land use possibilities range from global trade facilities and industrial development to hotels, tourism, and recreation.

The Port of Corpus Christi is doing all this while continuing to focus on its core business. Tonnage records consistently surpass those set the previous year, and, with its central location in the Americas, those increases should continue for years to come.

The Port is centrally located for trade between North and South America, provides access to a land bridge between the Caribbean and the Far East, and is the closest port to Los Angeles and Monterrey, Mexico, from Caribbean and many South American countries.

Or, as they say at the Port of Corpus Christi: "The 21st Century Will Move Through Us." ■

Cruise ships translate into diversification for the Port of Corpus Christi. The visit by the M/S ARKONA marks the beginning of the Port's efforts to attract the cruise industry to South Texas.

CORPUS CHRISTI

Regional Transportation Authority

Some people might argue that the Regional Transportation Authority's value to the community can best be measured in dollars and cents. After all, the RTA, which provides bus service to an 830-square-mile area, has pumped tens of millions of dollars into the economy.

But others point to less tangible ways to measure its contribution. Founded in 1986, the RTA also has improved public safety, enhanced the quality of life, and fostered a sense of community throughout the Coastal Bend.

Although bus service has been a part of Corpus Christi since 1925, it wasn't until 1985 that voters in Nueces and San Patricio counties established the RTA. To this day, the RTA, funded largely by a half-cent sales tax, continues to provide quality, accessible, and affordable transportation to Nueces and San Patricio counties.

The RTA has proven to be an indispensable cog in the region's economic machinery. More than 70 percent of the RTA's riders depend on bus service to get them to school, work, medical appointments, and shopping.

The RTA's 300 employees and contract personnel provide transportation to approximately 6 million passengers via bus, trolley, van, tram, and harbor ferry. Ridership has increased every year since 1988, even as administrative costs have declined.

In addition, the RTA's Care-B service provides transportation for people whose disabilities prevent them from using the RTA's regular routes. Before the RTA was established, people with disabilities lacked access to public transportation. Since its inception, Care-B trips have increased from 30,000 to more than 200,000 annually. This service eventually will decline as city buses are becoming capable of handling riders with disabilities.

The award-winning Staples Street bus transfer station incorporates community-decorated tiles that depict familiar images of Corpus Christi.

Along with dozens of bus routes, the RTA operates and maintains bus stops, van pools, passenger shelters, transit stations, and park and ride facilities, which transport workers to and from Naval Air Station-Corpus Christi and the Corpus Christi Army Depot.

The RTA does its part to promote tourism by operating the Harbor Ferry between the south side of the Corpus Christi Ship Channel and Corpus Christi Beach. Many tourists enjoy the RTA's scenic trolley along the Corpus Christi Bayfront and find its Corpus Christi Beach tram a convenient way to visit the many tourist attractions there.

The RTA works to be a good corporate citizen by collaborating with non-profit agencies and schools to provide safe and affordable transportation to special events. The RTA also offers local agencies and their customers temporary transportation assistance through its RTA Token Program and works closely with the "Welfare to Work" initiative.

Although most of its expenses are funded through sales taxes, capital expenses, such as the recent construction of four transfer stations, are funded largely by federal grants, which make up 80 percent of costs. The RTA has received national awards for projects such as the Staples Street Transfer Station and the design of bus stops along the Staples Street corridor.

As for the future, the RTA plans to continue on its current path of improving efficiency, enhancing services, and upgrading technology. ■

RTA's fleet of buses, trolleys, and a harbor ferry travels throughout an 830 square miles radius that translates into approximately 5 million miles a year.

U.S. Cellular

The Corpus Christi area is among a growing number of communities to benefit from U.S. Cellular's commitment to unparalleled customer service and generous community involvement.

This Chicago-based wireless telecommunications firm is deeply committed to its customers and to the communities it serves. Its dedication has made U.S. Cellular the nation's 11th largest wireless telecommunications provider and one of the fastest growing companies in the United States. The company has already topped the two-million-customer mark and expects to reach three million before the year 2001.

U.S. Cellular built its customer base by focusing its resources on small- and mid-sized cities like Corpus Christi. The company's investment in South Texas includes numerous retail outlets to provide customers with products and services in convenient locations.

U.S. Cellular has several stores in Corpus Christi and in communities throughout the Coastal Bend, including Victoria, Alice, Kingsville, Beeville, and Rockport. Additional stores are located in Laredo, Del Rio, Eagle Pass, and Uvalde.

U.S. Cellular managers make many business decisions locally. Corporately, the company recognizes the importance of developing its services based on the needs of the individual communities it serves. In the same way, decisions about community involvement are made at the local level. This allows U.S. Cellular to participate in a wide range of community programs.

U.S. Cellular is especially fond of its relationship with James W. Fannin Elementary School. In 1997, the company "adopted" Fannin's students and teachers through the Corpus Christi Business Alliance Adopt-a-School program. In the past years, U.S. Cellular has funded several projects, including enhanced landscaping and an upgrade to the school's science lab. U.S. Cellular associates enjoy participating in a variety of Fannin programs throughout the school year.

In June 1999, U.S. Cellular partnered with the Junior League of Corpus Christi and the Corpus Christi Parks and Recreation Department to expand KidsPlace Unlimited, a popular bayfront park. The expansion project drew upon the skills of thousands

(from left) Linda Marroquin, U.S. Cellular Sales Support; Jettie Powers, Junior League Sponsorship Chairwoman with daughter, Grace; and Lori Dellinger, U.S. Cellular Market Manager with daughter, Shelby celebrate the completion of the KidsPlace Unlimited's expansion project.

(from left) Andy Banda, Portland Senior Sales Associate; Sally Mungia, Retail Sales Supervisor; and Michael Manschot, Retail Sales Manager welcome customers to the grand opening of the Portland store located at 1500 Wildcat Drive.

of community volunteers who came together for a week-long construction project that resulted in a larger playground that is accessible to children and parents of all abilities.

1999 also marked the inaugural year of the U.S. Cellular U.S. Open Windsurfing Regatta. The regatta is a weekend-long, free-to-the-public event held in Corpus Christi Bay each May. U.S. Cellular sponsors the regatta to reward the customers and the community it serves with a fun, family outing.

U.S. Cellular is proud to support many South Texas service organizations including American Red Cross, Muscular Dystrophy Association, United Way, Corpus Christi Campus Crime Stoppers (a project of the Corpus Christi Crime Stoppers, Inc.), and Bayfest.

Corpus Christi's U.S. Cellular market also participates in community service programs developed at the corporate level and implemented in U.S. Cellular markets nationwide. An example of these programs is S.A.F.E. (Stop Abuse From Existing), an award-winning partnership with women's shelters to provide wireless phones to victims of domestic violence.

Other examples include H.O.P.E. (Homeless Outreach Phone Effort), which provides free long-distance calls to the homeless during the holidays, and Opportunity Calls, an effort to give homeless individuals private voice mailboxes where prospective employers and landlords can leave messages.

Another program, Cellular S.T.A.R.S. (Student Training and Rescue Sessions), teaches children in grades K through 3 how to use a cellular phone in emergency situations, and C.A.L.L. (Community Action Life Line) provides postal carriers, school crossing guards, and campus crime patrols with wireless phones so they can report unusual activity or emergencies.

Valuable services, commitment to customer relationships, and a focus on community involvement make U.S. Cellular the way people talk in Corpus Christi. ■

SOL Communications

SOL Communications is dedicated to providing customers the most advanced wireless communications services at affordable prices. To accomplish this goal, it brought to South Texas the first GSM network, the world standard for wireless communications, providing greater call clarity, more flexibility, and advanced calling management features.

GSM (Global System for Mobile Communications) is the leading wireless digital technology in the world. With networks in 129 countries, GSM is used by more than 150 million subscribers worldwide, with 3.5 million users in 44 states and more than 3,500 cities.

SOL Communications has created simple, value-priced calling plans without the hassle of long-term contracts. The first minute of all incoming calls on the SOL Communications network is free, and SOL Communications offers free long-distance calls from a SOL Communications wireless phone to anywhere within its service area. SOL Communications makes long distance affordable with low rates to anywhere in the United States and Mexico from SOL's local coverage area.

Its advanced call management features include caller ID, call waiting, conference calling, call forwarding, voice mail, and text messaging.

SOL Communications is also committed to providing superior wireless PCS communications throughout South Texas, offering more services and features at affordable prices.

SOL Communications has built the largest digital coverage area within the South Texas region, representing a combined population of more than 2 million people. With its GSM network, customers gain the advantages of the most advanced digital technology available in the marketplace today.

SOL Communications is the first PCS company in South Texas to employ SIM "smart card" technology to offer more personalized phone features and improve phone security. This allows SOL Communications to provide the most advanced wireless voice and data communications services available.

Smart cards are inserted into the caller's phone and authorizes them to use the GSM network. The smart card is one of the security devices on the GSM network that makes it difficult to steal numbers or make fraudulent calls. It also contains all of the customer's personal information and phone settings.

GSM simplifies wireless data communications to allow laptop and palmtop computers to be connected to GSM phones. GSM enables SOL Communications to provide integrated voice mail, high-speed data, fax, paging, and short message services through a single phone.

SOL Communications offers customers a wide variety of small, lightweight phones that sport a selection of stylish looks and a diverse set of features. Built-in features, such as phone books, alarm clocks, calculators, fax, auto redial, and even games, allow callers to select the best communications tools to fit their active lifestyles.

SOL Communications offers phones from famous name manufacturers, including Nokia, Ericsson, and Motorola. It also offers a full selection of accessories including extended-life batteries, chargers, hands-free car kits, carrying cases, and custom-colored faceplates.

GSM companies have created more than 12,000 new jobs in the United States and Canada, with an estimated 30,000 new workers involved in service, manufacturing, and associated jobs. SOL Communications has contributed to those numbers, bringing more than 125 new jobs to the South Texas market.

SOL Communications—a retail store at Huntington Square.

Southwestern Bell

Southwestern Bell Telephone has called Corpus Christi home since 1891, when Southwestern Telephone and Telegraph bought out Corpus Christi Electric Company's telephone exchange. Today, Southwestern Bell offers a wide range of telecommunications services to its customers, including local and long-distance phone service, wireless communications, data communications, paging, high-speed Internet access, cable and satellite television, and security services. As a subsidiary of SBC Communications, Inc., Southwestern Bell answers the call for residential and business customers.

Southwestern Bell employees have an average of over 21 years of experience. Pictured: Santiago Solis and Manny Esquivel, III, cable splicing technicians.

Southwestern Bell Today

With more than 38,000 employees in Texas, Southwestern Bell has invested nearly $1 billion annually to expand and enhance the state's infrastructure with the latest technologies. This infrastructure includes more than 9.3 million access lines and assets valued at $18 billion.

Each year in Texas, Southwestern Bell employees generate more than $1.3 billion in payroll and its 23,100 retirees draw more than $179 million in pension, resulting in a total impact of more than $500 million.

Products and Services

Southwestern Bell continually develops products, services, and applications to enhance life. Residential services include Caller ID, CallNotes, Call Waiting, Call Waiting ID, Call Forwarding, and Internet access. Key business applications include telecommuting, PC faxing, desktop videoconferencing, telemedicine, and distance learning.

In addition, Southwestern Bell develops and provides many state-of-the-art telecommunications technologies. By the year 2002, 80 percent of all Southwestern Bell customers will have access to Digital Subscriber Line service in Texas. DSL technology expands the amount of data that can be transferred over a traditional copper phone line, allowing for high-speed Internet and data access and other services.

Directory Advertising and Publishing Services

Southwestern Bell Yellow Pages provides advertising services and annually publishes 177 directories in Texas. The Corpus Christi Bay Area Directory includes Yellow Pages, White Pages, money-saving coupons, government listings, an events calendar, area attractions, and other helpful features. The company also delivers product samples, fliers, magnets, and other items to new residences and businesses, and coupons to targeted audiences at strategic times throughout the year. SMARTpages, an Internet website providing business and listing information, is the latest offering from Southwestern Bell Yellow Pages, the industry leader in bringing advertisers and consumers together.

Wireless and Internet Services

Southwestern Bell Wireless is a leading wireless provider, serving 10.1 million customers and 119 markets nationwide, including 9 of the nation's top 10 markets. Southwestern Bell offers extended home calling areas and one-stop shopping for all wireless services, including messaging and prepaid services.

Southwestern Bell Internet Services is the nation's eighth largest Internet service provider, offering a range of simple, affordable, and reliable Internet access services to business and residential customers.

Community Focus

Southwestern Bell emphasizes community partnerships through the Southwestern Bell Pioneers, employees and retirees who annually volunteer 3.4 million hours throughout Texas. Efforts center on education, including Operation SchoolNet, a program to wire more than 260 schools for Internet access.

Southwestern Bell and the Southwestern Bell Foundation give millions of dollars annually to promote education, economic development, health and human services, and cultural diversity. Southwestern Bell invested $14 million in non-profit organizations last year, and paid nearly $740 million in local and state taxes.

As these initiatives demonstrate, Southwestern Bell, with its more than 100-year history in Corpus Christi, remains committed to the communities where its employees live and work. ■

Southwestern Bell provides state-of-the-art digital technology for all communication needs. Pictured: Jeff Jung, director of external affairs.

11
chapter eleven

Manufacturing & Distribution

Horton Automatics, 106
Occidental Chemical Corporation, 107
DuPont, 108

Photo by Bryan Tumlinson.

Horton Automatics

Chances are good that you encounter a Horton Automatics product almost every day of your life without ever realizing it.

This Corpus Christi-based firm, a division of the Overhead Door Company of Dallas and a subsidiary of Sanwa Shutter of Japan, makes automatic doors, revolving doors, and automatic windows used at airports, hotels, restaurants, and other public buildings all over the world.

They're the kind of products most people take for granted, and yet our lives would be much more difficult without them.

This Corpus Christi-based firm, which remains relatively obscure even in its hometown, is a world leader in the automatic door industry. The company has 130 distributors throughout North America who sell and service Horton Automatics products.

Horton Automatics accounts for approximately 25 percent of the U.S. market for automatic doors, revolving doors, and automatic windows. Its Telford, England, plant, which opened in the late 1980s, assembles and sells Horton Automatics products in Europe.

Corpus Christi residents Dee Horton and Lew Hewitt, who co-founded the company, invented the automatic sliding door in the 1950s while working at Horton Glass Company. They came up with a solution to a problem that plagued Corpus Christi and other windy cities: automatic doors that swung outward often wouldn't open in 20 to 30 mile-per-hour winds.

The solution? An automatic sliding door.

With Hewitt's mechanical aptitude and Horton's salesmanship, the two men founded Horton Automatics in 1960 and began convincing store owners, architects, and construction contractors to try their new product.

Sales grew and continue to do so today. The company's 15 percent average annual growth rate allows the company to double sales every five years. In 1990 sales surpassed the $22 million mark; in 1999 sales topped $60 million.

Horton Automatics, inventors of sliding glass doors, make approximately 25 percent of automatic doors sold in the United States. Customers include the Denver International Airport (above), McDonald's, Toys R Us, and Disney World.

Horton Automatics manufactures the largest and most complete line of revolving doors and entrances in the industry.

You can go almost anywhere in the world and find a Horton Automatics product.

They can be found—among many other places—at Toys R Us, Universal Studios, McDonald's, Disney World, Dallas-Fort Worth Airport, The National Assembly in Seoul, Korea, Moscow State Bank in Russia, and the French side of the tunnel beneath the English Channel.

Horton Automatics installs about 32,000 products each year. They include automatic sliding doors for pedestrian use, automatic swinging doors used in grocery stores, and automatic swinging doors that work like a normal door or open automatically with the push of a button. They also make automatic and manual revolving doors, security revolving doors that restrict unauthorized traffic or verify when an authorized user passes through, and automatic windows for drive-through restaurants. They also manufacture a small line of industrial doors used in clean rooms, manufacturing plants, and other industrial facilities.

The company manufactures all of its products at its Corpus Christi plant, where it employs more than 300 hourly employees and approximately 85 salaried employees. Its Telford, England, plant, which assembles products from parts shipped from Corpus Christi, employs another 50 people.

The company plans to continue its practice of using profits to finance growth, with the goal of expanding sales throughout the world. So next time you encounter a door or window that moves on its own, whether it's in Corpus Christi, Texas, or Kuala Lumpur, Malaysia, chances are it will be a Horton Automatics product. ∎

Occidental Chemical Corporation

Occidental Chemical Corporation (OxyChem) is a classic example of a company that strives to improve the lives of its employees, customers, and neighbors. Though its name is not generally seen on retail-store shelves, its products are widely used, and its philosophy of business and citizenship benefits millions of people every day.

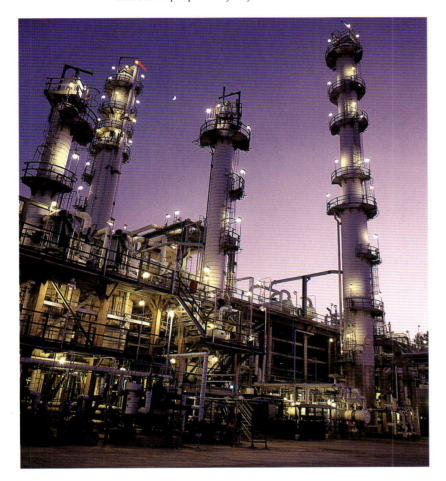

The Ingleside plant produces products which are used to purify our water, protect our crops, and build our homes.

OxyChem is one of the world's largest commodity chemical producers, with interests in basic chemicals, petrochemicals, polymers, and specialty chemicals. OxyChem has annual sales of about $3 billion, employs about 6,000 people, and operates about 40 manufacturing sites worldwide.

One of its sites is in Ingleside, Texas. OxyChem acquired the Ingleside facility, located a few miles north of Corpus Christi, in 1987, and refurbished it to restart production in 1988. The facility produces chlorine, hydrogen, caustic soda, ethylene dichloride (EDC), vinyl chloride monomer (VCM), electricity, and steam. All of this means little to most consumers until they consider what an important role these products play in their everyday lives. If you have gone swimming, driven a car, or washed clothes this week, you have probably used products from OxyChem. Among other things, OxyChem products make it possible for us to clean our bathrooms, purify water, fertilize our gardens, protect our crops, produce paper, clothing, pipe, and wall coverings, and light our homes.

OxyChem's Ingleside facility is now one of the busiest in the Port of Corpus Christi. Some 200 ships are loaded at its docking facilities each year, with approximately 75 percent of the plant's product headed for overseas.

With a deep commitment to safety, environmental, and health, OxyChem has taken a leadership position in response to environmental concerns about chemical production and has consistently achieved one of the best safety records in the industry. In fact, it has been honored with 27 OSHA Star sites (the highest achievement in safety presented by the Occupational Safety and Health Administration), the Ingleside facility being one of them.

OxyChem is committed to helping people, improving their quality of life, and making each community in which it operates a safer, cleaner, better place. At the Ingleside facility, OxyChem and its employees support the United Way, American Heart Association, the National Conference for Community and Justice, along with many other charities. It also takes part in the "Adopt A School" program, having adopted Stephen F. Austin Elementary and Sheldon Blaschke Middle Schools, where many employees work with students who need academic help.

OxyChem employs more than 450 local people at its Ingleside site.

CORPUS CHRISTI

DuPont

The motto adopted by employees at DuPont's Corpus Christi Plant perhaps best describes this 1,109-acre manufacturing facility: "People, Quality, Safety & Environment."

This simple motto has far-reaching implications for employees, customers, and nearby residents, who count on DuPont to produce high-quality products in a safe, clean environment.

Tank cars, columns, and storage spheres provide an interesting background for the main entrance building to DuPont's "OSHA STAR" Corpus Christi Plant.

Employees at DuPont's Corpus Christi Plant, which started up initial facilities in 1973, manufacture hydrofluorocarbons (HFC-134a and HFC-152a), hydrochlorofluorocarbons (HCFC-124), and a co-product, hydrogen chloride, at this state-of-the-art facility.

DuPont led the way in producing these environmentally friendly chemicals as an alternative to chlorofluorocarbons by opening the world's first HFC-134a plant in December 1990, and now operates the largest commercial-scale HFC-134a facility in the world.

Products made at the Corpus Christi Plant have enhanced the lives of millions, providing products used in home refrigerators, automotive air conditioners, pharmaceuticals, industrial chillers, aerosol propellants, insulating foams, and commercial refrigeration.

Although the market has changed drastically over the past 25 years, DuPont employees have responded to the challenge thanks to a work environment designed by the company to encourage employees to do their best. DuPont believes a work environment that creates spirit, mutual respect, and trust promotes a learning culture that capitalizes on the diversity of all employees and consistently yields excellent results.

A key ingredient in this formula is safety. DuPont's goal each year is to record zero injuries, illnesses, or incidents at its Corpus Christi Plant—a goal that is achieved on a frequent basis. DuPont also has participated in the OSHA Voluntary Protection Program and has been certified a STAR site since February 1984, one of only a handful to have received its fourth consecutive recertification.

DuPont has achieved this stellar performance and safety record while driving toward its goal of zero emissions. During its history, DuPont's Corpus Christi site has reduced its total site emissions from more than 1,500 tons per year to less than 50, and the quest toward "zero" continues.

DuPont's impact on the local environment can be measured in economic terms as well. Employment as of June 1999 stood at 199 operations personnel and 75 contractor personnel with an annual payroll of more than $12.3 million. Each year the plant spends approximately $3.3 million in taxes, $7.2 million on utilities, and $10 million in local purchases.

But DuPont's contribution to the community can be measured in human terms, too. DuPont employees volunteer their time to such groups as the San Patricio County Local Emergency Planning Committee, two area chambers of commerce, and the San Patricio County Economic Development Corporation.

The plant has served as a Pacesetter Company for the United Way of the Coastal Bend and is paired with Cunningham Middle School under the Adopt-A-School Program and with Ingleside High School and Gregory-Portland High School for the Junior Achievement program. In addition, the plant has an active Community Advisory Council, which provides a forum for open communication between plant representatives and the community.

Through hard work, Corpus Christi Plant employees have achieved high standards of performance and business excellence. With a continued commitment to their core values of safety, health, and environmental excellence; high ethical standards; and a work environment that is conducive to each employee contributing to their maximum; excellence will be sustained.

DuPont has successfully operated as a company for almost 200 years and will continue to provide value through "The miracles of science" to improve and enhance life on our planet. ■

A Production Technician completes a final safety inspection of a tank car before releasing it for shipment to a customer.

Photo by Bryan Tumlinson.

12

chapter twelve

Business & Finance

Corpus Christi Chamber of Commerce, 112-113
City of Corpus Christi, 114-115
Hilb, Rogal and Hamilton Company, 116

Photo by Bryan Tumlinson.

Corpus Christi Chamber of Commerce

The Corpus Christi Chamber of Commerce is the premier business advocate in the Texas Coastal Bend, facilitating business-to-business growth, community expansion, and leadership development.

It is the largest business organization in the region, with more than 1,600 members backing this important group, which has played an important role in making Corpus Christi the economic,

Corpus Christi Chamber of Commerce Annual Banquet.

cultural, and political hub of the Coastal Bend. Its efforts began shortly after its inception when it set about convincing the U.S. Congress that Corpus Christi would be a perfect site for a deep-water port. The Port of Corpus Christi opened on September 14, 1926, paving the way for the area to become a major center for oil refining and petrochemical manufacturing.

Their work pays dividends to this day. The Port of Corpus Christi is now the sixth largest port in the nation, generating 9,000 direct and 31,000 indirect high-wage jobs.

The Chamber's efforts later expanded to include completion of the 2-mile-long seawall to protect the city's downtown from flooding and storm damage caused by hurricanes. The 1919 hurricane devastated the city, killing 287 people and wiping out the tourist industry. In 1940, a $2.5 million bond issue supported by the Chamber funded completion of the 14-foot-tall structure 20 years after it began.

The Chamber of Commerce was instrumental in other improvements to the city's infrastructure such as the Harbor Bridge, completed in 1959 to allow automobile traffic to flow over the Corpus Christi Ship Channel without interruption from ship traffic; the Nueces Bay Causeway, linking Corpus Christi to its neighbors to the north; and the John F. Kennedy Causeway, connecting Corpus Christi with Padre and Mustang islands to the south.

The Chamber of Commerce also contributed to developing Corpus Christi as a strong military town, leading the way in bringing to the area Naval Air Station Corpus Christi, Corpus Christi Army Depot (a repair center for rotary wing aircraft) and Naval Station Ingleside, home to the Navy's mine warfare fleet, and the Intracoastal Waterway, a canal-like system of waterways running along the U.S. coastline from the Canadian border to the Mexico border.

The Chamber also has contributed to making Corpus Christi the educational hub of the Texas Coastal Bend, supporting local educational institutions such as Del Mar College, Texas A&M University-Corpus Christi, and Texas A&M University-Kingsville.

The Chamber recognizes the importance of recreation to local residents and the value that the area's natural beauty has to the community and to the millions of tourists who visit here each year. To that end, the Chamber has taken an active role in preserving the area's natural beauty while enhancing the public's enjoyment of it. The Chamber played a leading role in securing the Padre Island National Seashore, the longest undeveloped barrier island in the United States; Mustang Island State Park, a 3,703-acre park overlooking the Gulf of Mexico; and the Texas State Aquarium, dedicated to the study of plants and animals native to the Gulf of Mexico.

The Chamber's role in promoting the region would likely please Corpus Christi's founder, Colonel Henry Lawrence Kinney, who as early as 1839 advertised internationally to attract settlers to the "Naples of the Gulf."

Many came, and by 1905, with a population of 6,900, the community formed its first authentic Chamber of Commerce—known as the Corpus Christi Commercial Club and later the Corpus Christi Commercial Association.

An aerial view of the Buy the Bay Showcase—an annual trade show sponsored by the Corpus Christi Chamber of Commerce.

PADRE ISLAND AND THE BAY AREA

In 1924, the newly formed Corpus Christi Chamber of Commerce agreed to assume the association's obligations, assets, responsibilities, and functions. Henry B. Baldwin, the Chamber's first president, declared to the Chamber board that "this group can do anything they set their minds on doing."

Baldwin was right, and the proof is in the city's growth and the numerous public improvement projects spearheaded by the Chamber over the years.

The Chamber acquired its first home in the early 1950s after raising $100,000 in contributions to fund construction at 1201 North Shoreline Boulevard. In 1981 a $600,000 expansion and renovation project doubled the size, providing space for the Corpus Christi Area Convention and Visitors Bureau and the Corpus Christi Area Economic Development Corporation.

The Chamber, reorganized, revitalized, and re-energized in recent years, continues to focus on creating links to the business community with an eye toward attracting future business.

The Chamber's vision statement declares that its purpose is to "promote and enhance business growth and prosperity," while its mission statement describes it as "a member-driven organization whose principle mission is to foster business growth by advocating business issues, enhancing the business climate, and providing services to our members."

The Chamber works hard to deliver a diversified program for its members by promoting member-to-member business, encouraging residents to buy Corpus Christi first and maintaining a strong legislative agenda on both local and state levels. It also

The Corpus Christi Chamber of Commerce.

has strengthened its relationship with a program designed to create future leaders and communicates with members using all forms of media. Those include the Chamber's web site, www.corpuschristichamber.org, a public access TV program, and a monthly membership newsletter.

The Chamber is actively building partnerships and coalitions with other entities in the community. It acts as a link between local businesses, between outside businesses interested in conducting commerce in Corpus Christi, and as a link to other institutions interested in promoting Corpus Christi as an economic hub.

The Chamber, which plays a supportive role in business recruitment by supporting small businesses interested in moving to the area, acts as a resource for existing and new businesses to expand or develop markets in Corpus Christi.

The Corpus Christi Chamber of Commerce remains a vital, active organization promoting the Corpus Christi area, serving the needs of the business community, and making Corpus Christi a better place in which to live.

One advantage of being a chamber member is having the opportunity to network with other members.

City of Corpus Christi

In 1519, on the Roman Catholic Feast Day of Corpus Christi, Spanish explorer Alonzo Álvarez de Piñeda discovered a lush semi-tropical bay on what is now the southern coast of Texas. The bay, and the city that later sprung up there, took the name of the feast day celebrating the "Body of Christ."

The spot Piñeda discovered is now home to the largest city on the Texas Coast and the sixth largest port in the nation. Key industries include petrochemical, tourism, health care, retail,

The Corpus Christi manager carries out policy and handles operations as directed by the city council.

education, shipping, agriculture, and the military. Since its incorporation in 1852, Corpus Christi has grown into a regional hub for marketing, processing, packaging, and distributing agricultural commodities for a 12-county trade area.

The city of Corpus Christi began as a frontier trading post, founded in 1838-39 by Colonel Henry Lawrence Kinney, an adventurer, impresario, and colonizer. The small settlement, hard-bitten and lawless, was called Kinney's Trading Post or Kinney's Ranch.

It remained an obscure settlement until July 1845, when U.S. troops under General Zachary Taylor set up camp there in preparation for war with Mexico. The Army remained until March 1846, when it marched southward to the Rio Grande to enforce it as the southern border of the United States.

About a year later, the city took the name of Corpus Christi because a "more definite postmark for letters was needed." It was incorporated on Sept. 9, 1852. Residents elected a city council and a mayor, Benjamin F. Neal, who served from 1852 to 1855.

The city charter, a document establishing a city's principles, functions and organization of its government, was adopted in 1876. The city's first ordinance, adopted January 15, 1879, made it against the law to let hogs and goats run loose.

Corpus Christi has a home-rule government with a mayor, eight council members, and a city manager. The city manager functions as the chief executive officer, carrying out policy and handling operations as directed by the city council.

In 1983, the city adopted single-member districts, which allow voters in a particular area to elect someone from their district to represent them on the city council. Five city council members are elected through single-member districts, while three others and the mayor are elected at-large. The city also has more than 40 boards and commissions that establish a direct link between citizens and the city council and staff.

The city of Corpus Christi provides a variety of facilities and services to the community, including police; fire and emergency medical services; health services; parks and recreation, which include youth and senior programs; a natural history museum; libraries; an airport; and marina. Other services include water, wastewater, gas, garbage, and brush collection, recycling, street maintenance, and traffic signs and signal maintenance.

The water department alone oversees more than 1,600 miles of water transmission/distribution mains and has a combined storage capacity of more than 16 million gallons. The wastewater department operates six treatment plants with a combined treatment capacity of 42.7 million gallons per day.

The city strives to be progressive in updating its infrastructure and planning for future resources by annually updating its comprehensive capital improvement program. The drought in

City Manager David Garcia is the city's chief executive officer. Among the city's responsibilities is maintenance and operation of the city marina, one of the city's most popular and beautiful amenities.

1996 brought statewide attention to water problems. The city, through an extremely effective regional partnership with the Nueces River Authority and the Port of Corpus Christi Authority, completed construction of the 101-mile Mary Rhodes Pipeline, which transports water from Lake Texana to the city's O.N. Stevens Water Treatment Plant. In addition, the Texas Natural Resources Conservation Commission approved the Garwood transbasin diversion as another water source proving that, through planning and cooperation, water can be secured for the region in record time.

While the city places strong emphasis on infrastructure and basic services, the organization also has a commitment to provide a variety of recreation and cultural amenities. Part of that commitment includes substantial funding for local arts organizations. Citizens and visitors can easily access any one of five libraries, or spend a fun and educational day at the Corpus Christi Museum of Science and History. Another beautiful and popular attraction has always been the bayfront marina, located a stone's throw from downtown Corpus Christi.

To ensure the continuity of quality services, the city follows sound financial policies and practices.

The city's fiscal year begins August 1 and ends July 31, and the budget is made up of six major funds. The General Fund pays for the administration of city government and traditional public services such as police, fire, streets, park and recreation, and solid waste services. The Enterprise Fund accounts for services

Corpus Christi has a home-rule government with a mayor, eight council members, and a city manager.

provided to the general public on a fee basis, including funds for aviation, ambulance, golf, marina, and utilities. The Internal Service Fund provides goods and services for other departments on a cost-reimbursement basis, including health insurance, maintenance services, and information systems. Other funds account for debt service, special revenues, and trusts. The city also provides funding and support to enhance economic development efforts.

Maintaining a safe community is a major priority for the city. The police and fire departments have established state-of-the-art communications systems and work closely with the county, the Local Emergency Planning Committee, and industries to be on top of any emergency situation. The Corpus Christi Crime Control and Prevention District, which uses sales tax revenues to fight crime, has in recent years enabled the city to increase its police force, equipment, and support personnel, especially targeting youth and neighborhood initiatives. In addition, the city's emergency medical services are ranked number one in the state, excelling in response time and patient survival rates.

The city of Corpus Christi constantly strives to continuously improve the programs and services it provides for local residents and visitors, with special importance placed on responsive customer service. In fact, the city's organizational goal is to be a national leader of excellence in public service. ■

The city places a strong emphasis on infrastructure and basic services such as street improvements, police, fire, park and recreation, and solid waste services.

Hilb, Rogal and Hamilton Company

The Corpus Christi office of Hilb, Rogal and Hamilton Company (HRH) has provided innovative insurance and risk management solutions to the South Texas community for more than 75 years.

Founded in 1923 as Wallace L. Dinn and Company Insurance, the firm merged with HRH in 1990, a move that enabled its experienced, knowledgeable staff to enhance its local expertise with the nationwide resources of one of the largest insurance intermediaries in the world.

As the only insurance agency in Corpus Christi with nationwide resources, HRH acts as an intermediary between clients and insurance companies to provide insurance contracts to individuals and a wide range of businesses. Whether a sole proprietor or a multinational corporation, all HRH clients share a common need: to identify and manage risk in their organizations and in their personal lives.

To that end, HRH advises clients on risk management techniques such as self-insurance, transferring risk to others, risk avoidance activities, claims analysis, and risk reduction through loss prevention, safety training, and engineering. Using a team approach to serving customers, HRH adds value in the critical issue of risk management in the lives and businesses of clients.

As an intermediary for clients (who are traditionally mid-sized businesses), HRH benefits both insurance companies and customers by offering a variety of competitive products from which they can choose. Clients view HRH as a technical resource they can call upon to assist with understanding their particular risks as well as the complexities of insurance policy terms and conditions. HRH negotiates competitive insurance policy terms and premiums and is a client advocate when a claim occurs.

Dave Cavenah, President and Loyd Neal, Chairman.

HRH sells a full range of insurance coverages: Personal lines (homeowners, auto, and life insurance), Employee Benefits (group health, disability, and corporate life insurance), and all categories of Business Insurance.

HRH is uniquely qualified to serve the South Texas community thanks to a talented pool of professionals on the local, regional, and national levels. HRH employees have earned numerous professional designations and a significant percentage have worked in the insurance industry for many years. HRH encourages continuing education among its employees enabling them to better serve their customers.

HRH also encourages employees to become involved in charitable and professional organizations and service to their community. An executive at HRH has served as Corpus Christi's Mayor; another has served as President of the Independent Insurance Agents of Texas.

HRH has laid a solid foundation for future growth allowing it to stay ahead of trends and capitalize on market opportunities. HRH is committed to continue providing insurance products and risk management solutions into the 21st Century.

Left to right: Murray Bass III, Judy Bergstrom, Wally Goodman, Alan Dinn, Leslie Robertson, Loyd Neal, Dave Cavenah, Claudia Lobell, Bryan Bergstrom, David Collins.

Photo by Bryan Tumlinson.

13

chapter thirteen

The Professions

Hunter & Handel P.C., 120-121
Naismith Engineering, Inc., 122
Collier, Johnson & Woods, P.C., 123
Richter Architects, 124
Fields, Nemec & Co., P.C., 125

Photo by Bryan Tumlinson.

Hunter & Handel P.C.

Politics and the law merge to create a force to be reckoned with at Hunter & Handel P.C., the self-styled "maverick defense firm."

As a Texas legislator, Todd A. Hunter pioneered legal reform in Texas. Now with his partner Rodney R. Handel, he's pioneering new ways for law to serve business. The two combined their legal expertise in March 1992, when they decided to form their own general litigation defense firm.

Located in the Tower II building in downtown Corpus Christi, Hunter & Handel handles civil defense cases, representing insurance companies and those they insure; corporations, banks, and governmental entities on issues such as slab foundation cases, insurance coverage, automobile injuries, and accidents; and professional and employer liability. Its clients include Farmers Insurance, The Hartford, Fireman's Fund Insurance Company, Lancer Claims Services, Prudential, Formosa Plastics, Koch Industries, the Texas Association of Counties, and Providian National Bank.

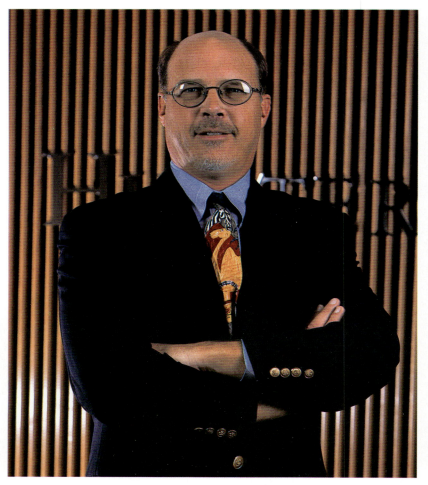

Rod Handel has successfully represented the firm's clients including Oxy Chemical Corporation, Valley Transit Corporation, Quaker Chemical Corporation, Amana Refrigeration, Inc., American Home Products, Farmers Insurance, Providian National Bank, ReMax Realtors, Texas Association of Counties, Aransas County, and Hidalgo County.

The firm is proud of its reputation for quality work, political contacts, and accessibility. It emphasizes teamwork, innovation, and personal contact with its clients.

"I want this law firm to be perceived as a trustworthy law firm. It's a hardworking law firm, and it's a politically connected law firm. And I think that's very positive," Hunter said.

Hunter, the senior partner of the firm, is best known for his leadership and accomplishments during four terms in the Texas House of Representatives. He received accolades from local, regional, and statewide groups for his commitment to causes such as tort reform, education, business development, and insurance reform. Hunter was also known for his ability to obtain bipartisan agreement while in the Legislature—a legacy he attributes to his upbringing, since his father was the Republican county chairman in Washington County, Oklahoma, and his mother, an English teacher, was a Democrat. He was frequently courted by members of both political parties to run for higher office, or to switch parties and run for a higher office.

Hunter, who was born in Bartlesville, Oklahoma, was admitted to the bar in 1978. He has been a certified civil trial lawyer in the State of Texas since 1983. He is a member of the Texas Bar

"We are probably the most unique firm in Corpus Christi," Hunter said. "We're the only defense firm in Corpus Christi with a partner who was in the Texas legislature, and I'm the only lawyer in Corpus Christi who lobbies."

Association, Nueces County Bar Association, Nueces County Young Lawyers Association, and the American Bar Association. Hunter's area of practice includes insurance, commercial, banking, tort trial and appellate practice, and mediation.

He was elected to the Texas Legislature in November 1988 and sworn in January 1989. During his four terms in the Texas House of Representatives, Hunter served as chairman of the House Committee on Civil Practices, which had involvement with the Texas Practice and Civil Remedies Code, and he was a member of the House Committee on Ways and Means. He also served on the following House committees—Appropriations (two terms), including one as the chair of the Subcommittee on Education; State Affairs, vice chairman; Elections, chairman of budget and oversight; Local and Consent Calendars; Urban Affairs; and Higher Education.

Hunter's legislative impact can be seen in many arenas. He was involved in statewide legislative initiatives such as civil justice reforms. He jointly wrote tort reforms dealing with medical malpractice, the liability of third parties whose connection to the case is questionable, punitive damages, frivolous lawsuits, whistleblower protection, and venue shopping.

He also wrote legislation that brought telecommunications and education together by unifying university systems' tele-education programs. And he passed a measure that repealed a two-year-old state mandate that exempted slab foundations 10 years old or older from homeowner insurance coverage. Hunter is also active in the community. He has been on the board of directors for the Corpus Christi Chamber of Commerce, serving as vice president and president-elect in 1987. He is also a graduate of the Leadership Corpus Christi Program, former board member of the Citizens Advisory Committee on Health and Welfare, and is involved in more than a dozen other organizations.

"We are probably the most unique firm in Corpus Christi," Hunter said. "We're the only defense firm in Corpus Christi with a partner who was in the Texas Legislature, and I'm the only lawyer in Corpus Christi who lobbies."

Hunter is one of several lobbyists for the City of Corpus Christi, pushing issues and promoting key legislation designed to benefit the Coastal Bend.

Hunter was the *Corpus Christi Caller-Times* Newsmaker of the Year for 1996. He has also been recognized by *Texas Monthly* magazine and the *Dallas Morning News* for his legislative accomplishments.

Hunter is married to Alexis Taylor and has three children, Todd Jr., Michael, and Christina.

Handel, who was born in Madison, Wisconsin, was admitted to the bar in 1986. A graduate of University of Wisconsin, Handel obtained his certified public accountant license in Illinois in 1981. He received his law degree at The University of Houston in

Gov. George W. Bush signs the punitive damages bill, jointly written by Rep. Todd Hunter, to applause by (from left) Lt. Gov. Bob Bullock, Sen. David Sibley, Rep. Todd Hunter, and House Speaker Pete Laney.

1986. Among his professional activities are membership in the State Bar of Texas, American Bar Association, Corpus Christi Bar Association, Corpus Christi Young Lawyers Association, and Texas Association of Bank Counsel.

He is licensed to practice in the Southern, Northern, and Western U.S. District Courts of Texas, the Fifth Circuit, and has practiced in federal courts in California and Connecticut. His area of trial practice includes insurance defense litigation, products liability, toxic torts, DTPA and consumer litigation, and employment law. Handel also is retained by insurance companies to render insurance coverage opinions.

Handel was married to his wife Maria in 1989 and has one son, Anthony. ■

Naismith Engineering, Inc.

You need look no further than the Corpus Christi Bayfront to appreciate the impact Naismith Engineering, Inc. has had on the South Texas landscape. The region's leading engineering firm has its roots in the construction of the 2-mile-long seawall that protects the city from devastating hurricanes.

Over the past half century, Naismith has taken part in many important public and private ventures, including local landmarks like Padre Staples Mall, The South Texas Institute for the Arts, Nueces County Showbarns, and Memorial Coliseum. The firm also contributed in the design phase of most of the warehouses along Agnes Street.

Local residents have come to count on Naismith to take a leading role whenever a major construction project is under way. And the firm itself seeks to abide by its mission statement: "To be the leading engineering, environmental and surveying consulting firm in South Texas…"

The firm was founded in 1949 by Conrad S. Blucher and James S. Naismith. The Conrad Blucher Institute for Surveying and Science at Texas A&M University-Corpus Christi is dedicated to Blucher, a third-generation surveyor whose family mapped much of Nueces County between the mid-1800s and 1954. In 1961, James P. Naismith, a son of James S. Naismith, joined the firm. He purchased Mr. Blucher's interest in 1968 and the name was changed to Naismith Engineers, Inc. He served as president of the firm until 1989. James S. Naismith continued to be active with the firm until his death in 1980. The firm was sold to several of the employees and re-named Naismith Engineering, Inc. The Naismith name is recognized throughout the United States for a vastly different reason. In 1891, James Naismith, James S. Naismith's father, invented the game of basketball in Springfield, Massachusetts.

Memorial Coliseum and portion of Seawall (1953).

Naismith boasts expertise in environmental issues, public works and infrastructure, structural and investigative engineering, land development, and surveying. It has designed and developed public water supplies which serve municipalities and industries located throughout South Texas. The firm has also developed wastewater treatment systems to enhance and protect local bays and estuaries, wastewater reuse programs, roadway improvements, and drainage and flood control systems.

Its 70 employees, in offices in Corpus Christi, Austin, Laredo, and Brownsville, play an important role in the future of South Texas, working with municipalities, industries, water districts, drainage districts, utility companies, school districts, and construction companies.

The firm continues to participate in the future development of South Texas through its support of Packery Channel and Island Beach Park, Sunset Lake, John F. Kennedy Causeway improvements, development of long term water supply, and civil work for the new federal courthouse.

But its work extends beyond the scientific and technical aspects of engineering. Naismith takes seriously its obligation to clients and the public and operates on the principle that client satisfaction is the key to building a successful consulting firm. The firm demonstrates its commitment by giving back to the community through support of local charities and participation in professional societies.

Its philosophy is exemplified by an excerpt from the American Society of Civil Engineers Manual "Consulting Engineering— A Guide for the Engagement of Engineering Services": "Upon engineers rests the responsibility for conceiving and designing all types of engineering works, and for providing the assurance that they are properly and economically constructed and used. The health, safety, and comfort of the public depends to a considerable extent upon how well the Engineer fulfills his obligation."

Coastal Bend Estuary (1998) Bay Debris Clean-Up Project.

Collier, Johnson & Woods, P.C.

Collier, Johnson & Woods addresses the concerns of the independent businessperson. While located in Corpus Christi, they serve a wide variety of clients located throughout the United States. Their roots go back more than 50 years. During that time, their basic philosophy has remained unchanged: treat each client as they would want to be treated and offer nothing less than excellence in every area of financial, tax, and management consulting.

CJW is a healthy, growing, and assertive firm, enthusiastically pursuing their clients' success by providing a full range of traditional accounting, auditing, and tax services, as well as progressive tax planning and management consulting services. They strive to provide professional services efficiently and effectively through their skilled and proficient owners' and staff's direct and personal attention to their clients' goals and strategies for achievement while retaining a local, personal atmosphere.

They've never been confined simply to numbers. More often than not, they find their role as business advisors expanding. That means developing client relationships not confined to professional designations, but driven by the need to constantly produce results. CJW's clients have come to appreciate their insight, experience, and even wisdom in giving advice and expertise where and when it counts the most. This requires that they maintain close and open relationships with each of their clients, who often look to CJW to go beyond the normal compliance matters and assist them in many important business and financial matters.

Today's opportunities and challenges require substantial examination, analysis, knowledge, and commitment. CJW is a needs-oriented service provider offering: specialists in governmental entities and industries such as financial institutions, construction and manufacturing, automotive, broadcasting, retail, wholesale, and distribution; experts in functional areas such as profitability, strategic planning, technology, estate and financial planning, and business valuations; and service teams developed to provide access to firm-wide and outside resources.

CJW is committed to its profession and community through active, leadership participation in such organizations as the Chamber of Commerce, United Way of the Coastal Bend, Consumer Credit Counseling Services, Texas State Aquarium, South Texas Food Bank, Corpus Christi Estate Planning Council, Rotary Club of Corpus Christi, and Junior League. They are a member of the Private Companies Practice Section of the American Institute of Certified Public Accountants, attaining the highest level of performance rating on each of their peer reviews. Their members play active roles in the Texas Society and Corpus Christi Chapter of CPAs.

As a local CPA firm, CJW realizes that the services they provide are only as good as the people they bring to their clients to guide and advise them. Their only product is the professional competence and motivation of their people. They provide jobs for local graduates who share their philosophy to aid in growing the Corpus Christi community and its businesses.

CJW strives to attract men and women who are academically strong, personally committed to their profession and community, and who want to help clients meet their goals. Every person that associates with CJW concentrates on servicing the closely held, usually family run business. They work as a cohesive firm, tapping into each other's areas of expertise as needed. Thus, CJW is a growing team of certified public accountants who are accomplished business advisors with a passion for helping entrepreneurial businesses succeed and providing the business community with timely, personal, and highly professional accounting services.

Seated left to right: Brigid W. Cook, Ernest L. Johnson;
Standing left to right: F. John Shepherd, John E. Porche,
Randy R. Vrana, and Laurie W. Cook.

Richter Architects

It's been said that buildings can say a lot about the people who create them. If that is true, then the buildings designed by Richter Architects of Corpus Christi, in teamwork with their clients, speak volumes about a commitment to community, to excellence, and to long-term value.

Richter Architects, 201 South Upper Broadway, is renowned for its ability to create innovative and inspiring designs while responding to budget challenges. In fact, virtually all of the many design awards earned by the firm have been in recognition of projects with modest budgets and everyday functional requirements. The firm is dedicated to the pursuit of thoughtful, functional, cost-effective, well-crafted, stimulating, and environmentally appropriate architecture.

Central to the Richter Architects' design philosophy is the commitment to look to the client and to the site for inspiration, not to themselves. In this manner, architecture can reflect the people who use the building, not the people who design it. Each project is as different as the site it sits on, the client who commissions them, and the dreams that inspire it. This diversity of work is among the things that set the firm apart. They believe that working in a broad variety of building types keeps fresh ideas flowing which lead to innovative and practical designs.

Such designs for university work include the Fine Arts Center for Del Mar College and the Texas A&M Corpus Christi University Services Center. Educational projects include Dawson Elementary School and additions to Ray High School, Wynn Seale Middle School, and Menger Elementary School. Religious projects include St. Mark's Episcopal Church, Grace Presbyterian Church, and additions to First Baptist and First United Methodist churches, and to the Church of the Good Shepherd. Urban and civic projects include the Water Street Market and the Port of Corpus Christi Waterfront Development.

Left to right: Architects Samuel D. Morris, AIA, Elizabeth Chu Richter, AIA, and David R. Richter, FAIA at the project construction site of the cruise ship terminal and conference center for the Port of Corpus Christi.

As protection of the environment continues to emerge as a major public issue, Richter Architects expands their professional capabilities to provide clients "green" architecture. The Mustang Island Episcopal Conference Center, designed to be carefully tuned to a sensitive barrier island site, was published nationally by the Department of Energy and Green Building Council in *Environmental and Economic Balance—A 21st Century Outlook* and has been noted by the State of Texas General Land Office as a model for environmentally conscious barrier island development.

The firm is directed by David R. Richter, FAIA and Elizabeth Chu Richter, AIA, who are both leaders in the community and in their architectural profession. David Richter, who began working in Corpus Christi in 1975, was inducted into the American Institute of Architects College of Fellows in 1994 as recognition of "his inclusive design philosophy and influence on South Texas architecture." He served as 1998 president of the Texas Society of Architects, the first architect from Corpus Christi to serve in that capacity. Elizabeth Chu Richter, who joined the firm full time in 1989, has twice served as chairman of the South Texas Public Broadcasting System and has produced a statewide radio program on architecture. In 1998, she received from the Texas Society of Architects the John G. Flowers award, granted in recognition of her "outstanding contribution in the public media to promote excellence in the built environment and to advance the architectural profession."

Great cities are built one building at a time and even the most modest structure is important to its own neighborhood. The professionals at Richter Architects are building a legacy of design excellence through service to clients who endeavor to build well, to create value, and to contribute to quality of life. ∎

National award-winning project: Brooks County Safety Rest Area designed by Richter Architects for the Texas Department of Transportation. Recipient of an Honor Award for Architecture from the American Institute of Architects.

Fields, Nemec & Co., P.C.

Fields, Nemec & Co., P.C. is much more than an accounting firm.

This Corpus Christi-based certified public accounting firm also provides customers with creative financial advice and good business survival skills that go far beyond basic tax compliance and accounting.

FNC offers tax planning, management advisory services, estate and financial planning, litigation support, evidence development, and expert witness testimony. They also counsel troubled businesses, assist lenders, provide organizational and management counsel for law firms and medical practices, and help design and install data processing and management information systems.

But their services don't stop there. FNC also offers recovery planning to help businesses survive disasters, identifies hidden causes for low productivity, develops management compensation plans and cost-effective ways to enhance benefit programs, helps businesses fill key positions, and assists family-owned businesses with management and ownership succession planning and conflict management in a family business environment.

How does a local CPA firm do all that?

With a highly trained and experienced team and the vast resources of the R.S.M. McGladrey network's national and international capabilities. The R.S.M. McGladrey network consists of almost 400 offices in more than 75 countries, making it the 10th largest accounting and consulting firm in the world, the 7th largest in the nation, and the largest national firm dedicated to serving family and privately owned businesses.

This affiliation with a national firm allows FNC to meet demands that financial services be performed by a "nationally recognized accounting firm" and is a natural outgrowth of FNC's commitment to clients and their determination to keep up with developments in accounting and consulting. This affiliate relationship allows FNC to retain its name, autonomy, and independence as a locally owned and responsive accounting firm responsible for its own client fee arrangements, delivery of services, and maintenance of client relationships.

The firm shareholders shown left to right; Dorothy Fowler, Robert Fox, Rudy Sturgeon, and Karen Denson.

The Company is located at 501 South Tancahaua Street. Fields, Nemec & Co. is located on the second floor.

FNC provides quality, creative, cost-effective accounting and consulting services to its diverse client base with special emphasis on industry niches, including construction, oil and gas, manufacturing, not-for-profit, medical, governmental entities, and farming. FNC pursues a climate that encourages professional growth by employing expertly trained people responsible for knowing the businesses in which their clients operate.

It is FNC's goal to use audit-related tasks as a springboard to providing solid business and financial advice. Their objective is to help business owners and professionals make money—and keep more of it—while scrupulously adhering to the highest ethical standards.

Personal attention is central to FNC's philosophy of providing the highest quality service to its clients. They believe in developing strong relationships with senior client management, which demands a high level of principal and supervisory involvement with every client.

FNC's commitment to excellence is demonstrated by its membership in the demanding peer review process implemented by the Division of CPA Firms of the American Institute of CPAs, founded in 1977 to promote excellence in the accounting and auditing practices of CPA firms. Every three years the institute sends in an audit team to evaluate the firm and express an opinion on its quality of work. FNC recently passed its sixth peer review.

Fields, Nemec & Co., P.C. care about success. Their diverse capabilities can be recognized within the multitude of services offered to clients. By working with a foundation of experienced professionals, FNC is able to devote themselves to problems which companies are unable to resolve on their own. Fields, Nemec & Co., P.C. work hard to ensure that business owners and professionals continue to profit both internally and externally despite the obstacles that finance and management can create.

14
chapter fourteen

Real Estate, Development, & Construction

Fulton Construction/Coastcon Corp., 128-129
Moorhouse Construction Company, 130
Wilkinson/Reed Development, Inc., 131
Prudential Real Estate Center, 132
Haeber Roofing Company, 133

Photo by Bryan Tumlinson.

Fulton Construction/Coastcon Corp.

Fulton Construction and Coastcon Corporation have done as much to change the South Texas landscape as anyone in this region's rich history. Since 1983 when the two companies formed a joint operating venture, this successful duo has completed more than 100 projects with a total worth of more than a quarter billion dollars.

Projects completed by Fulton/Coastcon, both singly and jointly, read like a "Who's Who" of important public and private buildings in the region. They include Kings Crossing Country Club, Texas State Aquarium, Corpus Christi Greyhound Race Track, Bay Area Medical Center, Spohn Hospital South, Spohn Surgical Center, Frost Bank, The South Texas Institute for the Arts, De Dietrich manufacturing center, the 16-screen Tinseltown movie theater, and Bonilla Plaza Office Building. One of their most recently completed projects is the new U.S. Federal Courthouse on Shoreline Drive.

They've also improved and expanded landmark facilities such as Padre Staples Mall, Moore Shopping Plaza, Sunrise Mall, Moody High School, and the Nueces County Jail.

Fulton/Coastcon is one of the nation's top 400 construction contractors ranked by dollar volume of construction work and is by far the largest contracting firm in South Texas. They've reached that status not only by combining their efforts, but by focusing on the Corpus Christi market and attracting repeat business through stellar customer service. Not only does Fulton/Coastcon honor the one-year warranty on its work, it also has been known to repair problems that crop up five or six years down the road.

Joe Fulton of Fulton Construction Corporation and Jim Barnette of Coastcon Corporation head Fulton/Coastcon. Both led established firms and had successful, independent careers before forming their joint venture, a decision that allowed them to maintain separate offices and businesses while combining opposing yet complementary strengths.

They came together to pool their financial and manpower resources to effectively compete with larger, out-of-town contractors. At the time, many local people perceived them individually

The Texas State Aquarium is a showplace to experience habitat and marine life of the Gulf of Mexico and the Caribbean.

as too small to handle the city's larger construction projects. Forming a joint venture convinced many that Fulton/Coastcon could handle virtually any size building project.

While Fulton specialized in winning contracts by submitting the lowest bid, Barnette negotiated contracts with owners without going through the bidding process. Negotiated projects are increasingly popular with private businesses (the bidding process must still be used in some public sector projects) because they give the owner more control. In the negotiation process, the owner takes an active role in the project and in choosing alternatives to control costs before the design is completed. This ensures that the architects and engineers will not have to rework the project when projected costs are too high.

Fulton won the lion's share of bid projects in town, while Barnette garnered most of the negotiated projects in the area. Forming a joint partnership to combine their separate strengths has paid off for Fulton, Barnette, and the community.

Fulton's long career in the construction industry began in high school and summers while studying architectural engineering at the University of Texas. He came to Corpus Christi upon the advice of a professor, who said the seaside community promised the most growth of any Texas city.

The "Miradores" are placed in eight locations along the Corpus Christi seawall and have become a popular place for weddings.

The 20-story Omni Hotel overlooks the Corpus Christi Bay and the marina.

Fulton serves on the board of directors of Cullen/Frost Bankers Inc., the San Antonio-based holding company of Frost National Bank, the largest independent bank in Texas. He also has served as a commissioner of the Port of Corpus Christi Authority and chairman from 1991 to 1996, and previously served as chairman of the Greater Corpus Christi Business Alliance. He also has served as president of the Associated General Contractors of America's Texas state building branch, president of the Corpus Christi Area Convention and Tourist Bureau, and chairman of the Corpus Christi Area Economic Development Corp.

Barnette, a civil engineering graduate of the University of Mississippi, spent 10 years as a design engineer for a major regional consulting firm before founding his own general contracting firm in 1973. Barnette has served as chairman of the Corpus Christi Chamber of Commerce, board member of the Greater Corpus Christi Business Alliance, chairman of the city of Corpus Christi ethics board, and chairman of the city's mechanical advisory board. Barnette serves on the board of directors of American Bank.

In the joint partnership arrangement, either Fulton or Barnette has primary responsibility for the project and keeps in touch with the owner regarding construction progress. Owners feel reassured knowing that one of the principals in Fulton/Coastcon is closely involved in the process.

Customers know that dealing with Fulton/Coastcon means they'll be dealing with local, experienced people who not only will be on the job today but well into the future. That's because turnover at Fulton/Coastcon is almost non-existent, with many employees marking 20, 30, even 40 years with their respective companies. Fulton/Coastcon seeks to hire people with ties to the community, people who are less likely to pick up and move after a few years on the job. They also keep employees by offering a good benefits package and by treating employees fairly.

Clients can also count on Fulton/Coastcon to hire dependable, well-qualified subcontractors who appreciate Fulton/Coastcon's reputation and strive to match its record for quality, dependable service.

Fulton/Coastcon can handle all types of construction projects, whether industrial, commercial, institutional, or health care related. Corpus Christi's recent boom in the healthcare industry has been particularly challenging to the construction industry. Contractors must find a way to work on a facility without shutting it down or interfering with the hospital's ongoing critical functions.

Fulton/Coastcon has shown several times over that it can handle such challenges as it continues to reshape the South Texas landscape into the next millennium. ∎

The South Texas Institute for the Arts, designed by Phillips Johnson, is a premier art museum that also is active in educational programs.

Moorhouse Construction Company

Moorhouse Construction Company, 5826 Bear Lane, is a local business with a regional scope, offering reliable, cost-effective construction services throughout Texas and the Southwest.

This Corpus Christi-based firm, with branch offices in Houston and Harlingen, is a general contractor specializing in the construction of commercial, institutional, and industrial buildings. Typical projects range from chemical laboratories to medical clinics, for a wide variety of public and private owners. These buildings, varying in size from 5,000-square-foot facilities housing the personnel and equipment to control an entire refinery to entire school campuses, are offered by Moorhouse in a variety of delivery methods. Moorhouse offers their customers a full range of options from simple lump-sum bids to turnkey design-build.

Moorhouse Construction provides a complete menu of services to owners throughout the construction process, including design/build construction, site location and evaluation, conceptual budgets, and detailed estimates.

Commitment to customer needs and attention to detail are among the reasons Moorhouse Construction has grown into a regional force. An emphasis on job safety, reinforced throughout the company's approximately 100 employees, is borne out in its outstanding safety record.

Chairman B.L. Moorhouse founded the firm in 1975 as a general contractor specializing in remodeling and other small projects. Five years later his son, Burt Moorhouse, who now serves as president, joined the company. Maggie Moorhouse serves as treasurer and president of Moorhouse Associates, a consulting firm specializing in integrated resource planning.

Moorhouse completed this award-winning central control building for Citgo's Corpus Christi Refinery.

For more than 20 years Moorhouse Construction has built process facilities, laboratories, administration buildings, control rooms, and other specialized structures for industrial owners. Along with offering turnkey construction, they also provide ancillary services such as process piping, electrical, mechanical, and digital electronic systems.

They understand industrial and governmental regulations, and their well-trained crews meet demanding schedules while providing customers with a stable, experienced, and careful staff.

In the commercial construction industry, Moorhouse Construction has the expertise to build everything from retail centers to distribution warehouses. Each facility, whether new, an addition, or a renovation, is cost-effective, functional, within budget, and on time.

This multi-dimensional company has demonstrated its ability to change with the times, providing safe, clean, and reliable construction services in the fast-changing medical/healthcare industry. From noise abatement and a clean work site to sensitivity to ongoing business activity, Moorhouse Construction provides a healthy working environment with minimal disruption.

Its understanding of budgets and timelines and an appreciation for blending strength and function with aesthetics and atmosphere has served the company well in the institutional marketplace. Moorhouse Construction prides itself on careful execution of every project, which range from banking centers and churches to governmental buildings and schools.

Moorhouse Construction Company is committed to making Corpus Christi its home because of the quality of life and its desire to build a better future for employees and the community.

Educational facilities are a growing market for Moorhouse Construction Company.

Wilkinson/Reed Development, Inc.

Corpus Christi residents Carole Wilkinson and H.A. Reed want to do their part to improve the quality of life in their city by creating unique, high-quality homes in beautiful surroundings. This mutual desire led them to combine their talent and experience, and in 1997 Wilkinson/Reed Development was formed.

Their first collaboration is The Haven Townhomes, a $3 million development featuring 32 high-end townhomes in Wood River, a premier residential subdivision in northwest Corpus Christi. Wilkinson and Reed have seen this townhome development through all phases, from initial planning to the successful completion of quality, aesthetically pleasing townhomes.

While developing The Haven Townhomes, Wilkinson and Reed became aware of the need for additional residential development in northwest Corpus Christi. Their search for a unique tract of land led to their development of Heather Ridge Estates, a country estate subdivision bordering the Nueces River. This subdivision is unique in that it features rolling hills and large trees, characteristics not commonly found in other areas of Corpus Christi. Through their vision and commitment to maintain the beauty of natural surroundings, they were able to achieve their goal of designing a subdivision that encourages unique, high-quality homes while maintaining the relaxed South Texas atmosphere.

Wilkinson/Reed Development, Inc.'s expertise lies in building custom homes. Each home is designed to reflect the individual homeowner's taste and personality. Wilkinson and Reed's partnership provides a unique combination of experience and talent that can be extremely beneficial to clients in creating their dream home—in the $200,000 to $1 million range.

H.A. Reed, a Corpus Christi native and custom homebuilder since 1980, is known for integrity of construction, creative interior finish-out, attention to detail, and custom woodwork. Over the years, his talents have become legendary, leading realtors and homeowners to market each of his homes as an "H.A. Reed home." Reed's construction experience allows him to move a project from the beginning stages of site work through all stages of construction, including supervising swimming pool construction and designing landscaping that reflects the character and personality of the homeowner and the newly constructed home.

Carole Wilkinson, a real estate broker with over 25 years' experience in the legal and title fields, guides clients through all facets of construction, from plan selection to assisting in interior finish-out, to ensure the process goes as smoothly as possible. She also assists clients with the documentation procedures involved in new construction, including the loan process, and keeps costs within budget.

Wilkinson, who relocated to Corpus Christi in 1993 from Fort Worth, soon became aware of the tremendous growth potential for northwest Corpus Christi and the need for managed growth. She immediately became active in the NorthWest Business Association, an organization that promotes business in Corpus Christi's northwest district. Soon after, she served a two-year term as President. Wilkinson's talent, experience, and dedication to community led to her appointment as a Board member of the Regional Transportation Authority, the Greater Corpus Christi Business Alliance, and the Council of Governments.

As the developments of The Haven Townhomes and Heather Ridge Estates reach completion, Wilkinson/Reed Development, Inc. is concentrating on custom home building while searching for future unique, aesthetically pleasing residential home sites. This desire to beautify the Corpus Christi landscape is a commitment to community from which all residents will benefit. ■

The Haven Townhomes, a $3 million townhome complex constructed by Wilkinson/Reed Development, is located in Wood River, a prestigious residential subdivision in northwest Corpus Christi.

This elegant custom home, constructed by Wilkinson/Reed Development, is located in their residential subdivision, Heather Ridge Estates.

CORPUS CHRISTI

Prudential Real Estate Center

The Rock of Gibraltar is a fitting symbol for Prudential Real Estate. "The Rock"—strong, stable and recognized throughout the world—represents what has become one of the most impressive real estate companies in North America.

With more than 1,400 offices and 37,000 sales associates, Prudential Real Estate combines local strength with international name recognition to set itself apart in the competitive real estate industry.

Jacqueline L. Svoboda, president and CEO of Prudential Real Estate Center of Corpus Christi, 14200 South Padre Island Drive and 5417 Everhart Road, recognized Prudential's value when she joined the network in 1992.

"Prudential gives us decades worth of name recognition and the vision of an industry leader," she says. "This, coupled with the extensive network of professionals who align themselves with the power of The Rock, allows us to provide uncompromised service to all our clients…"

Only those companies that measure up to Prudential's demanding criteria may become part of the network. Prudential Real Estate Center, which covers the entire Corpus Christi Bay Area, is consistently ranked among the top ten real estate companies in Corpus Christi.

Svoboda, who owns the company with her husband, Henry D. Svoboda, began her real estate career in 1966. She has served as a Corpus Christi Board of Realtors director and is one of the few brokers in Corpus Christi to hold the distinguished CRB designation. Her daughter, Misty Svoboda, serves as relocation director, and her son-in-law, Jeff Young, as manager of the rental management division.

Although they proudly represent clients with homes of all sizes, they are known by many for their Fine Homes Division, which handles a majority of the area's more expensive houses, including most waterfront properties in the area.

Prudential also helps vacationers find a place to stay through the Prudential Resort Property Network. The network for both renters and buyers helps people find nice homes in which to vacation or relocate.

226 Augusta, Portland, Texas. Interior living area.
Photo by Art Carroll.

Prudential Real Estate and Relocation Solutions, the first fully integrated real estate and relocation service company in the industry, serves more than 900 corporations and institutions in North America.

Prudential's reputation helps network members attract the top real estate professionals in each market as evidenced by Prudential Real Estate Center's agents holding many prestigious designations in their field.

But what really sets Prudential apart from competitors is the world-class technology available to sales associates. Its eCertified sales representatives are technologically enabled to use all the high-tech resources available in the system. Its Intranet site, PREA Center, features news, information, marketing materials, and other tools to give Prudential listings an advantage.

Prudential sales representatives also benefit from Prudential's website which receives thousands of visits each week and provides direct links to affiliate companies.

But Prudential Real Estate Center realizes it takes more than technology to make a satisfied customer. Their goal is to provide an uncompromising level of personalized service in the hopes of securing customers for life. ■

226 Augusta, Portland, Texas. House exterior on the water.
Photo by Art Carroll.

Haeber Roofing Company

In 1978, while working at an Austin roofing company, Butch and Irene Haeber found themselves at a crossroads. They could either go to work for a roofing company in another state or return to Corpus Christi to start a roofing business of their own.

Butch, a Corpus Christi native, and Irene, a longtime resident, decided to return home to open Haeber Roofing Company in June of that year, despite a troubled economy and fears about starting a new business.

They began with a 5,000-square-foot warehouse, 600-square-foot office, and fewer than 10 employees. Now, more than two decades later, Haeber Roofing Company, 2833 Holly Road, is the largest roofing company in Corpus Christi, boasting a 30,000-square-foot warehouse, 3,500-square-foot office, and approximately 50 employees.

Like many successful family-owned businesses, the Haebers attribute their success to hard work, quality workmanship, and customer service.

Butch, a Corpus Christi native, supervises the fieldwork, while Irene handles the office. They're joined in the business by their daughter, Sharon Rucker, and her husband, Don Rucker III, a certified engineer. Sharon oversees the company's accounting department, while Don serves as operations manager, project supervisor, and estimator.

Haeber Roofing installs all types of commercial, industrial, and institutional roofing, and also installs residential roofing, mostly in custom homes where quality workmanship is the top priority.

They offer a wide range of roofing materials, including built-up, modified bitumen, single-ply, tile, metal, composition shingle, and wood shingle. They also provide water proofing at construction sites and coatings to preserve and protect existing roofs. Their custom sheet metal shop allows them to give customers less expensive, more precise, and better quality sheet metal than those found at building supply shops.

Their customer list looks like a "Who's Who" of Corpus Christi's public and private entities. They include the City of Corpus Christi, Regional Transportation Authority, Naval Station Ingleside, Corpus Christi Independent School District, Reynolds Aluminum, Koch Refining, Spohn Hospital, and Columbia Northwest Hospital.

Haeber Roofing serves a 150-mile radius of Corpus Christi, including San Antonio, Laredo, the Rio Grande Valley, and Victoria.

As the area's largest roofing company, Haeber Roofing is able to keep up with the latest developments in the industry, allowing employees to be among the most productive installers in the industry. Meanwhile, Don Rucker, as a registered engineer, is able to oversee projects that other companies can't handle with in-house staff.

The company and its customers also benefit from experienced and well-qualified employees who have stayed with the company since its inception. "When we hire someone, they stay," Irene said. "We provide them with above-average wages and a full benefits package. We operate like a family, and they're a part of it."

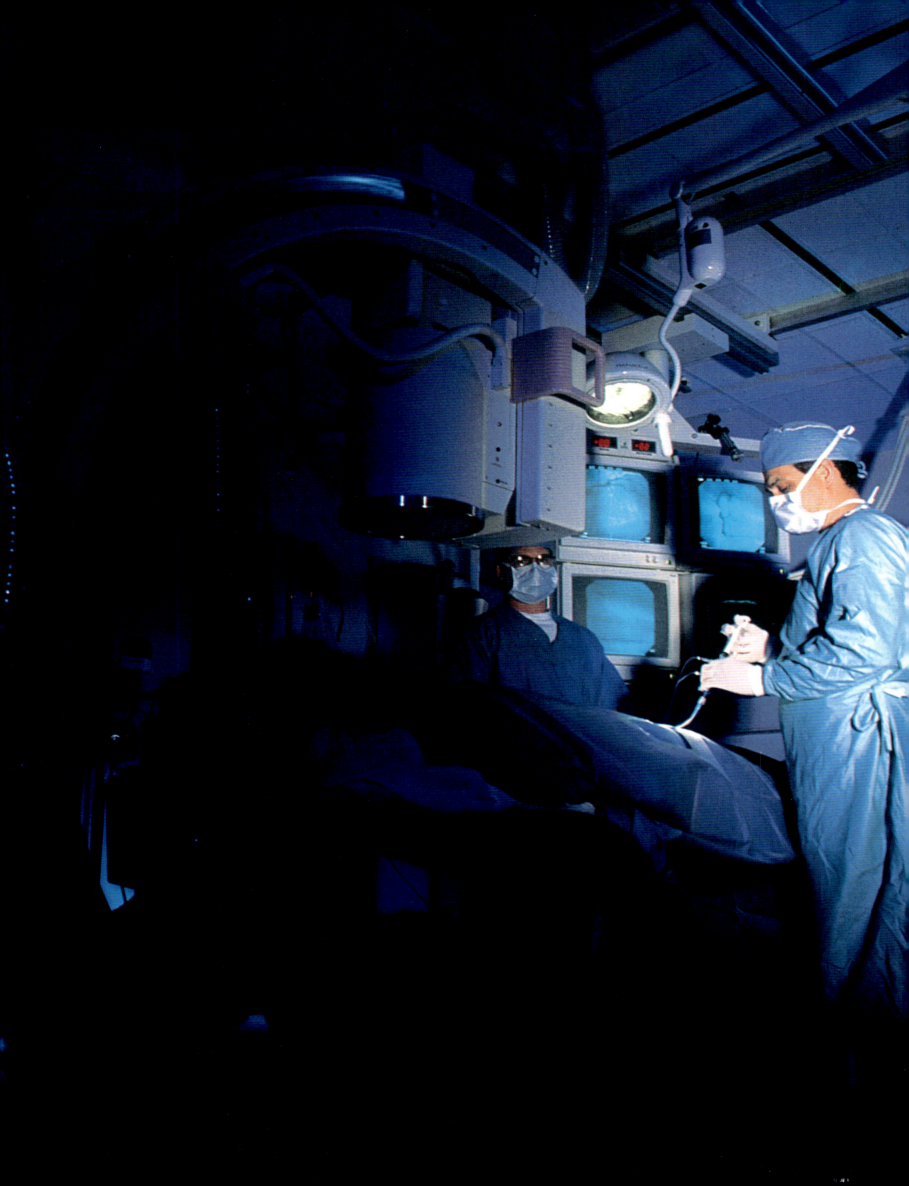

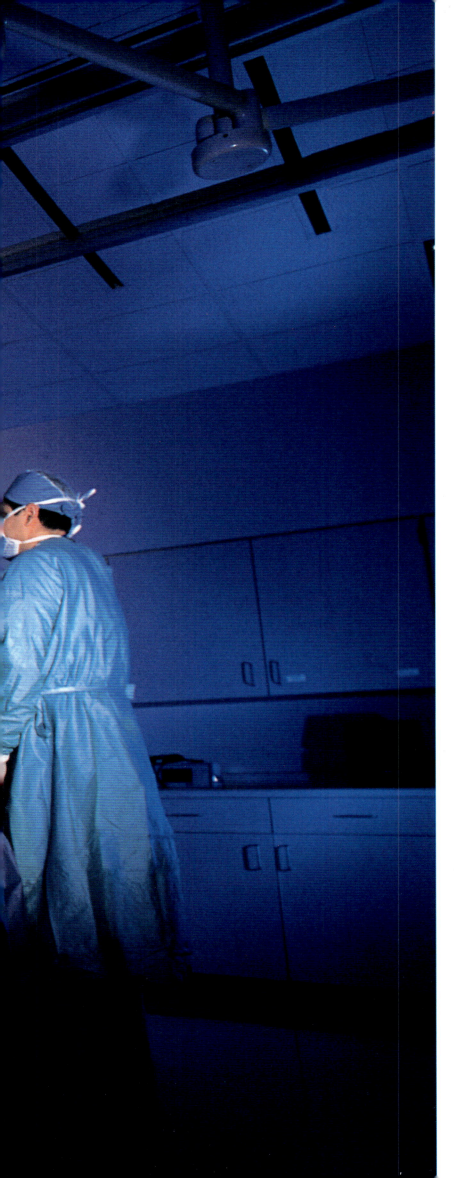

15
chapter fifteen

Health Care

Driscoll Children's Hospital, 136-167
Surgicare of Corpus Christi, 138
Corpus Christi Medical Center, 139

Photo by Bryan Tumlinson.

Driscoll Children's Hospital

No one cares more for children than Driscoll Children's Hospital of Corpus Christi. And that's exactly how Clara Driscoll, the granddaughter of a Texas patriot, envisioned the hospital when she requested that her estate be used to build and operate a children's hospital here.

Her vision, along with that of Dr. McIver Furman, led to the opening of the hospital in 1953, through the Robert Driscoll and Julia Driscoll and Robert Driscoll, Jr. Foundation. The hospital is dedicated to providing the best care to all children, with respect and dignity, through a dedicated, compassionate health care team.

Driscoll Hospital is a special place, an institution of caring that has grown and improved throughout the years. This tertiary care regional referral center has pediatric board-certified specialists in 19 medical and nine surgical specialties.

Its health care providers understand that each child is a different, precious masterpiece in the making, and that the care of their health is one of the highest callings to which a person can strive. They also know that children require a wider range of supplies, special skills, extra caution, and more time from health care givers.

The hospital's referral area covers 33 counties of South Texas, a 31,000-square-mile area larger than the state of South Carolina. Each year more than 6,000 children are admitted to inpatient care, 5,000 patients for surgery, and 50,000 children for outpatient primary and specialty care. Driscoll was the first hospital in South Texas to provide emergency services exclusively for children. Today, it provides emergency care to more than 40,000 children each year.

Driscoll's specialized intensive care units offer the latest state-of-the-art services and technology to care for newborns, infants, and children with life-threatening illnesses and injuries. Its staff is represented by more than 200 pediatricians, pediatric surgeons, and other pediatric specialists.

They also boast a state-of-the-art ground/air transport team, an expertly-trained intensive emergency care team, a dedicated pediatric support staff, a renowned pediatric residency program, and specialized medical outreach and children's advocacy programs.

The hospital also has 200 licensed beds, a 20-bed pediatric intensive care unit, 40-bed neonatal intensive care unit, 12-bed

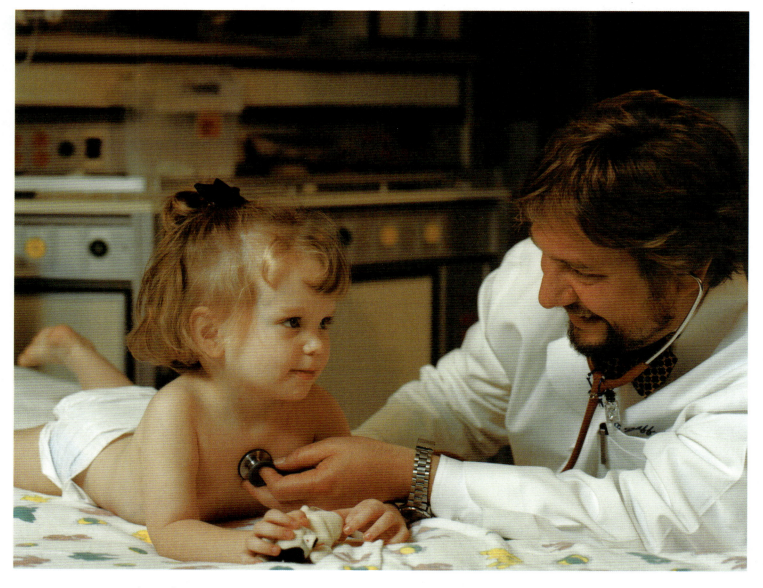

Dr. Mark Morales gives a Driscoll patient the care she needs.

Driscoll Children's Hospital.

neonatal intensive care unit at Spohn Hospital South in Corpus Christi, pediatric subspecialty clinics throughout South Texas, eight surgical suites, pediatric cardiology clinics, comprehensive medical and surgical services, a child protection team, Texas A&M University affiliation, and accreditation with the Joint Commission on the Accreditation of Healthcare Organizations.

The Driscoll Children's Hospital logo exemplifies the hospital's dedication to caring for children while honoring its South Texas roots. The "Y" in the logo is a bold, stylized version of the original Driscoll cattle brand, and the circle signifies dedicated continuity of care. In combination, the two form the image of a child with outstretched arms seeking help and recovery through faith and hope. The dimensional image of a child's building blocks symbolizes the unified comprehensive care offered by its staff, who assist physicians in the building of healthy futures for the children and adolescents served by Driscoll Children's Hospital. ■

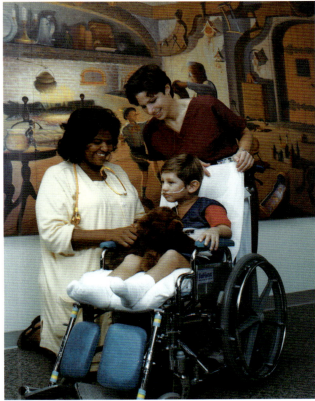

Dr. Stephanie Ried is part of the Driscoll team that makes childrens' lives better on a daily basis.

Surgicare of Corpus Christi

Many types of surgery have become so non-invasive that a hospital stay is no longer required. And in Corpus Christi, many elective, outpatient surgeries are performed away from the hospital in a state-of-the-art facility specializing in surgical procedures.

Surgicare of Corpus Christi located on Elizabeth Street.

Surgicare of Corpus Christi, 718 Elizabeth Street, is a licensed, accredited surgical facility established by concerned physicians who envisioned providing healthy individuals with a choice on where to go for elective, out-patient surgery. Surgicare, established in 1981 as the first organization of its kind in Corpus Christi, remains a competitive provider of outpatient surgical care in the Coastal Bend.

Providing more than 4,000 surgeries a year, Surgicare affords patients the same level of care for elective, outpatient surgeries as the larger hospitals in town. It does so by keeping up with the latest trends in surgery and anesthesia and by requiring continuous education for physicians and staff.

Surgicare of Corpus Christi is part of Columbia/HCA Healthcare Corporation's Ambulatory Surgery Division. With more than 75 similar surgical centers all over the nation, Surgicare benefits from a vast network of trained professionals who perform thousands of surgeries each year. Quality issues, continuing education and training, and new techniques in outpatient surgery and anesthesia are just a few of the many resources available within Columbia's Ambulatory Surgery Division.

With four operating rooms and eight recovery units, Surgicare provides complete peri-operative care from a streamlined admissions process to a recovery period that reflects each patient's individual needs. For those patients requiring an extended recovery, Surgicare provides ACLS-trained nurses who stay with patients at all times, allowing the patient to recuperate in the comfort and privacy of an extended recovery room.

Surgicare specializes in outpatient surgery, including ophthalmology, orthopedics, gynecology, podiatry, plastic, reconstructive or cosmetic surgery, ENT, urology, and pain management procedures. Outpatient surgery is primarily for healthy patients undergoing an elective procedure, although there may be occasions in which surgeries are diagnostic in nature or done to repair conditions such as certain broken bones.

Whatever brings you to Surgicare, you can be certain that the staff is well-trained and suited to take care of any needs that may arise. Our goal is to provide surgical services as part of an integrated healthcare system, while enhancing a patient's lifestyle. We hope to accomplish this by providing the surgical intervention that the patient's physician has determined to be necessary to return or elevate the patient to an acceptable level of functioning. This would enable the patient to perform activities that are necessary to meet their individual standard of living that only they can define, as their needs are uniquely theirs and may be different from patient to patient.

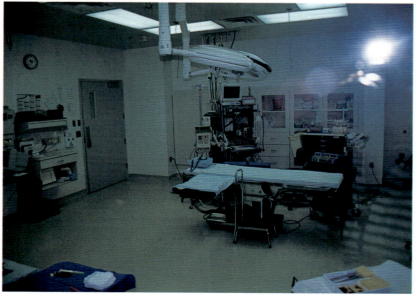

Operating room suite.

Corpus Christi Medical Center

As the largest hospital in the Greater Corpus Christi Bay Area, the Corpus Christi Medical Center is poised to offer a full range of healthcare services with outstanding clinical care, superior technological care, and comforting, reassuring personal care.

This 478-bed hospital employs approximately 1,400 people, including 700 active physicians, at its three campuses and, along with its extensive network of services and professionals, provides quality healthcare to all patients, making it the preferred healthcare resource in South Texas.

The Corpus Christi Medical Center is part of the Columbia/HCA Healthcare Corporation family. And, like a family, each of its three campuses—Bay Area, Doctors Regional, and The Heart Hospital—possesses different areas of expertise, including inpatient, outpatient, and special programs.

Bay Area—Corpus Christi Medical Center, 7101 South Padre Island Drive—houses a medical education residency program, the Breast Center of South Texas (a dedicated breast care diagnostic center), comprehensive nursing services, a 24-hour emergency room, and a women's services department with gynecological surgery and labor-deliver-recovery-postpartum suites.

Doctors Regional—Corpus Christi Medical Center, 3315 South Alameda Street—is a full-service, acute-care hospital offering a full range of inpatient and outpatient services, including

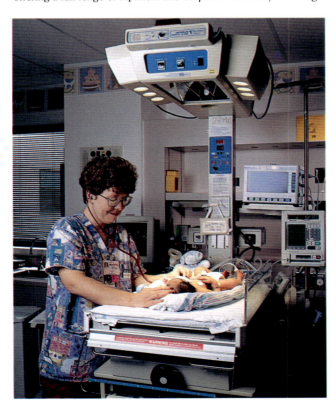

The Level III Neonatal Intensive Care Unit (NICU) is uniquely equipped and staffed to provide urgent and specialized care for critically ill and high risk newborns.

The Heart Hospital, adjacent to the Bay Area Campus on Corpus Christi's south side, opened its doors in January 1998.

a 24-hour emergency room, state-of-the-art cardiac cath lab, and a neuroscience program offering stereotactic procedures for non-invasive brain surgeries. It's also home to a neonatal intensive care unit, MRI diagnostic center, sleep laboratory, conference center, women's pavilion, and diabetes education center.

The Heart Hospital—Corpus Christi Medical Center, 7002 Williams Drive—is the first and only hospital in the area dedicated solely to cardiovascular procedures. Opened in January 1998, the Heart Hospital offers cardiac catheterization laboratories, state-of-the-art operating rooms, coronary care beds, telemetry beds, non-invasive diagnostic facilities, and a fully equipped fitness center.

Corpus Christi Medical Center also offers an array of other specialized services including:

• Cardiac Rehabilitation—available at the Heart Hospital for post-surgery patients on an inpatient and outpatient basis. Specially trained cardiac rehab professionals work individually with patients for maximum recovery.

• FirstSteps—a family focused maternity education program providing classes that prepare expectant families for pregnancy, birth, and parenting.

• Senior Friends—a national membership organization for those 50 and better. Senior Friends offers educational seminars, support services, health screenings, and assistance with insurance filing as well as exercise classes and opportunities for travel.

• Diabetes Care of South Texas—a diabetes management education program for people with either Type I (insulin dependent) or Type II diabetes. Diabetes management classes are available for patients and their families. Diabetes Care at Corpus Christi Medical Center has been awarded recognition by the American Diabetes Association in accordance with the National Standards for Diabetes Self-Management Education Programs.

16

chapter sixteen

The Marketplace, Hospitality, & Tourism

Whataburger, Inc., 142-145
Corpus Christi Convention &
Visitors Bureau, 146-149
Marina Grand Hotel, 150-151
Ramada Inn Bayfront, 152
Pagan-Lewis Motors, Inc., 153
Christy Estates Suites, 154

Photo by Bryan Tumlinson.

CORPUS CHRISTI

Whataburger, Inc.

When Harmon A. Dobson opened his first hamburger stand in 1950, he launched a Texas fast-food tradition that has become as familiar and as welcome as a South Texas sunset.

In that original wooden burger stand—with a working area of 10-by-23 feet—Harmon Dobson sold the basic Whataburger, cold drinks, and potato chips. The price was 25 cents for a burger. His journal records that demand even on the first day far outstripped his expectations. Soon afterward, he wrote in his diary, "Whataburger will probably turn out to be my 'life work.' I'm beginning to like and appreciate the business."

Harmon Dobson, a bush pilot, was very creative at promoting his new business—he towed bright-red "Whataburger" banners behind his single-engine Piper "Super Cub," blowing a big air horn that sounded like a duck honking. He dropped coupons and leaflets from the plane, inviting folks to the restaurant. Harmon Dobson also decided that his burgers needed to be larger than the standard four-inch buns, and arranged with Rainbo Bread Company to manufacture pans for five-inch buns. Harmon Dobson's thinking was that in Texas, where people think big, the Whataburger really needed to be large—to make people exclaim, "What a burger!"

Through his hard work and ingenuity, Harmon Dobson managed to turn Whataburger into the hamburger of choice for Texans, who consistently rate it their top burger choice. There are now more than 560 Whataburger restaurants throughout eight states and in Mexico. The distinctive restaurants feature an orange-and-white striped roof and offer a variety of products.

Where it all began! Harmon Dobson's first Whataburger restaurant circa 1950.

But the mainstay of the menu continues to be the signature product, a grilled quarter-pound, all-American beef hamburger on a five-inch bun with lettuce, three slices of tomatoes, four dill pickle slices, chopped onions, and mustard.

The Whataburger difference at its core is the quality of its food and the people that prepare it. The company, in its advertising campaigns, openly acknowledges that its customers don't want the fastest or lowest priced product. The Whataburger is famed for its taste and freshness, and every burger is made to order. Billboards extol the Whataburger virtues with subtlety and quiet confidence; one such message reads, "You could get a cheaper burger. But then you'd have to eat it." The corporate slogan is: "Real food. Real fresh. For Real folks. Since 1950."

Rapid expansion marked the growth of Whataburger, even from its earliest days. Just three years after Harmon Dobson began selling his distinctive version of the fast-food burger, the first Whataburger located outside of Corpus Christi was opened. Harmon Dobson's fourth burger stand was placed in nearby Kingsville, Texas, in 1953. That same year, Joe Andrews of Alice received the first Whataburger franchise.

In 1959, the company made its first steps outside the Lone Star State. The 21st Whataburger restaurant was opened in Pensacola, Florida. In 1961, Harmon Dobson built the first three-story, A-frame building with an orange-and-white striped roof that has become familiar to many Texans. The design of the restaurant has not only served as a visual billboard, with its distinctive orange-and-white stripes, but is in fact recognized as a pop icon of the 1960s. Today, most of the buildings retain the orange-and-white roof, while also reflecting the local architectural style.

The signature product. The Whataburger: a 5-inch bun, 1/4 lb. of all-American beef, three tomatoes, four pickles, mustard, lettuce, and onions.

A snapshot from the early years that borrows from the old adage, "It's not whether you win or lose, it's where you eat afterwards that's important."

The key to success has been the company's loyal customers and the Whataburger team members whose dedicated service keeps them coming back. There are hundreds of stories about Whataburger fans who have had Whataburger sent to them out-of-state via Federal Express; transplanted Texans whose first meal when they returned home was at a Whataburger; soldiers headed off to boot camp opting for a last meal at Whataburger; and more. On Valentine's Day in 1996, 24 couples were married at a Whataburger restaurant.

"We are successful because we have maintained a consistent focus on the fundamental principles that have made the company a Texas icon. And that is to serve our customers a fresh, made-to-order meal in a family atmosphere at a fair price," said Tom Dobson, president and CEO. "We never set out to be the biggest hamburger chain. We just wanted to be the best."

Most recently, the company opened its flagship restaurant, "Whataburger by the Bay," on Corpus Christi's main thoroughfare, Shoreline Drive, directly across from the Corpus Christi Bay. This restaurant, the corporation's

It was in 1972 that the company hit the 100 mark, opening its 100th restaurant. In 1979, the restaurants began serving breakfast in all locations. By 1978, Whataburger opened its 200th location. It reached 300 stores in 1980 and 500 in 1995. The stores also began 24-hour operations in all locations in 1982. In 1992, the business expanded into Mexico, making it a truly international phenomenon.

Founder Harmon Dobson died in a plane crash in 1967, and his wife, Grace Dobson, took over the business. In 1994, his eldest son, Tom Dobson, took over as company president and CEO. Believing that the company had lost focus, Tom Dobson immediately went to work restoring the original vision for Whataburger: to provide outstanding service and top quality, made-to-order food for a satisfied customer. He spent his first year as President and CEO assembling a new, streamlined management team and implementing an aggressive "back to basics" approach. The following year, overall sales jumped 5 percent and another 10 percent the year after that, earning Whataburger the number one ranking in same store sales growth by the Nation's Restaurant News.

Under Tom Dobson's leadership, Whataburger has not only rebounded, it's thriving in the most competitive sector of the restaurant industry. Despite its growth, the company remains family-owned and still retains the same principles on which it was founded. Its headquarters is proud to call Corpus Christi its birthplace, the city that has nurtured and supported Whataburger since those early days. And the company returns the favor by its active involvement and financial support of a wide range of community activities.

Harmon Dobson outside of one of his original restaurants.

Future generation of Whataburger fans.

Whataburger flagship dubbed "Whataburger by the Bay" sits proudly on Corpus Christi Bay.

largest, encompasses 6,899 square feet. The two-story building's architecture features the distinctive A-frame wrapped with a modern building that delivers beautiful views of the water and marina. Its menu offers premium items such as cappuccino and other gourmet coffees, the Whatachill (a slushy), soft-serve ice cream, and root beer floats.

Founder Harmon Dobson is immortalized at this restaurant as well, with a bronze statue of him on a park bench at the restaurant's bayside entrance. "The fact that Whataburger chose to build its flagship in Corpus Christi is testimony to the company's commitment to the people of our hometown," says Whataburger's Chief Operating Officer Tim Taft.

"There's no doubt that if we had built this restaurant in Dallas or Houston, we could have expected a greater financial return as well as increased exposure for our company on a national stage. But if we were going to have a flagship restaurant, the Dobson family was committed to it being in our hometown. It's where we got our start and it's a way of saying thanks for the special partnership we have enjoyed with our neighbors during the last 50 years."

PADRE ISLAND AND THE BAY AREA

Distinctive orange and white stripes on the Whataburger A-frame.

The year 2000 marks not only the first 50 years of Whataburger, it also finds the company positioned for the future. In a time when many companies would be enjoying such a milestone, this family-owned and operated business has rededicated itself to being the best hamburger company in the industry.

"We have advantages the large majors don't," says Dobson. "We are not part of a nameless and faceless conglomerate. Being family-owned gives us a corporate culture of family and, in turn, a closer relationship with our customers and team members. We're also quick. We can respond to changes in the marketplace rapidly and with smarter programs that actually reflect the needs and wants of our guests."

Whataburger means many things to many people and generations have come to enjoy what is called "The Whataburger Difference." It's a company that's proud of its heritage and especially proud to call Corpus Christi home.

Corpus Christi National Headquarters.

Corpus Christi Convention & Visitors Bureau

For years, Texans have been drawn to the Coastal Bend's pristine beaches, abundant wildlife, and friendly people. Now, the rest of the world is discovering them, too, along with the area's exciting tourist attractions, burgeoning nightlife, and profusion of water sports.

The Coastal Bend is a world-class destination without the crowds and high prices found in other places. It covers a wide and diverse area from Corpus Christi and the nearby barrier islands to Victoria 80 miles to the north and Kingsville 35 miles to the southwest.

In the Coastal Bend, you'll find something for everyone, whether it's shopping, nightlife, and the arts, or relaxing on the beach, deep-sea fishing, or marveling at the endangered whooping crane in its winter feeding grounds. Corpus Christi serves as the region's centerpiece with more than 250,000 people, the fifth largest port in the nation, and a bayfront whose beauty is unsurpassed.

The city of Corpus Christi chose this majestic backdrop for the Mirador de la Flor memorial on the seawall to honor slain Tejano singer Selena Quintanilla-Perez, a Corpus Christi native on the verge of crossing over into English-language recordings when she was killed by her fan club president in 1995. Her death at age 23 inspired a Hollywood movie starring Jennifer Lopez and Edward James Olmos.

If nightlife is your thing, check out Corpus Christi's Chaparral Street. This historic district a few blocks from Corpus Christi Bay has experienced a renaissance in recent years, with nightclubs and restaurants transforming this abandoned district into the city's late-night hotspot.

Shoppers will find much to enjoy in the Coastal Bend. The region's retailing hub is centered along Corpus Christi's South Padre Island Drive, where you'll find two malls, several shopping centers, and dozens of individual stores and restaurants.

Corpus Christi offers visitors the opportunity to participate in an array of fun recreational activities, including horseback riding on the beach. With warm weather nearly the entire year, Corpus Christi is a perfect vacation spot.

Nature's abundance attracts many to the Coastal Bend, home to two national parks, several state and local parks, sparkling bays and waterways, excellent deep-sea fishing, and one of the best birding sites in the nation.

Each year, birders flock to the Coastal Bend in search of the almost 500 species of birds that can be found here. Dozens of spots throughout the area are included in the Great Texas Coastal Birding Trail, a 500-mile path designed to guide birders to the state's diverse avian population.

Anglers enjoy deep-sea fishing and excellent bay fishing in the Coastal Bend, casting their lines for record numbers of redfish, speckled trout, and black drum. Port Aransas is one of the state's premier offshore fishing sites, with more than a dozen tournaments and countless guides and charter services.

The Deep Sea Roundup and Boat Show, a fishing tournament sponsored by the Port Aransas Boatmen Association, is the oldest fishing tournament along the Texas coast. This tournament pays champions cash prizes and trophies for the largest fish caught in several categories.

Duck, dove, and quail hunters find plenty of opportunities here, too. Many local residents have private leases on South Texas ranches, while others take guided tours or try their luck on public lands. Hunting lodges offer packaged hunts for duck, dove, quail, feral hogs, or deer.

The study and preservation of Coastal Bend nature include:

Padre Island National Seashore

This national park near Corpus Christi is one of the longest stretches of primitive, undeveloped ocean beaches in the United States. The national seashore is home to white sand-and-shell beaches, picturesque dunes, grassland, and tidal flats.

The USS *Lexington* is one of Corpus Christi's most popular attractions. Located next to the Texas State Aquarium, visitors can visit two of the state's top attractions in one place.

These beautiful Miradores Del Mar (Spanish for overlooks by the sea) are eight gazebo-like designs copied from similar structures in Morocco, Mexico, and Spain. Each Miradore has a bench, a water fountain, and a plaque dedicated to different milestones in Corpus Christi history. They represent the largest private gift to the city.

Texas State Aquarium

This four-story aquarium is dedicated to the study of plants and animals native to the Gulf of Mexico. Exhibits feature sand and nurse sharks, moray eels, barracudas, tarpon, tropical fish, and other sea creatures in several small tanks and two large tanks, including a 132,000-gallon aquarium. The aquarium also features a touch tank, and exhibits featuring sea turtles, North American river otters, and alligators.

• Aransas National Wildlife Refuge: This 70,504-acre wildlife refuge 35 miles north of Rockport is home to the endangered whooping crane. Facilities include a 16-mile paved road, Wildlife Interpretive Center, 40-foot observation tower, walking trails, and a picnic area.

• Corpus Christi Botanical Gardens: This 180-acre site features more than a thousand native plants. The Orchid House is home to the Larkin Orchid Collection, one of the largest collections in the Southwest with some 2,100 varieties.

• Hummer/Bird Celebration: Rockport celebrates the annual migration of thousands of hummingbirds with a festival packed with lectures, workshops, and field trips.

• Kemp's ridley Sea Turtle Restoration and Enhancement Project: Scientists formed this program in 1978 to help the endangered Kemp's ridley sea turtle by forming a secondary breeding population on Padre Island. Visitors can watch as biologists release turtle hatchlings into the Gulf of Mexico each summer.

• The University of Texas Marine Science Institute: Learn about Gulf of Mexico marine life, plants, and oceanography at this Port Aransas laboratory and research facility.

Preserving and honoring local culture is important to Coastal Bend residents, as evidenced by the number of museums in the area.

Corpus Christi Museum of Science and History

At the Corpus Christi Museum of Science and History, you can learn about Columbus's voyages and their impact on the New World in "Seeds of Change," a Smithsonian Institute exhibit on permanent display. The museum also houses artifacts from three Spanish galleons that wrecked on Padre Island in 1554.

John E. Conner Museum and King Ranch Museum

The John E. Conner Museum in Kingsville is designed to preserve the social, political, and natural history of the area and to interpret the bicultural heritage of the borderlands. The King Ranch Museum, also in Kingsville, is home to custom-made automobiles, saddles, guns, and antique carriages.

Texas Maritime Museum

The Texas Maritime Museum in Rockport is dedicated to preserving and interpreting the rich maritime heritage of Texas. Exhibits cover everything from the early days of French and Spanish exploration to the modern search for offshore oil and gas.

USS Lexington Museum

The USS Lexington Museum is one of World War II's most decorated aircraft carriers. The *Lexington*, decommissioned and serving as a floating museum off Corpus Christi Beach, served longer and set more records than any carrier in U.S. Navy history.

The area also honors the arts through several organizations such as:

• Ballet Nacional: This dance company strives to promote and preserve the area's Latin cultural heritage. The company stages two annual productions, *Noche de Gala*, an elaborate and formal show performed each winter, and Summer Salsa.

Padre Island National Seashore stretches 80 and one-half miles long. It is one of only eight national seashore areas in the country. Year-round activities include camping, picnicking, boating, surfing, swimming, beach combing, hiking, fishing, and bird watching.

- Cathedral Concert Series: Top-notch music staged in one of the area's most significant architectural achievements makes the Cathedral Concert Series a unique experience. The series, held at the Corpus Christi Cathedral, has featured the Vienna Boys Choir, the Roger Wagner Chorale, the Tommy Dorsey Orchestra, and the London Brass.
- Corpus Christi Ballet: This group has attracted several well-known ballet companies such as Mikhail Baryshnikov's White Oak Project, Stars of the American Ballet, and Ballet Stars of Moscow. The ballet holds special performances for children, and lectures and demonstrations on school campuses.
- Corpus Christi Concert Ballet: This small ballet company performs several productions each year, including educational ballet matinees of *The Nutcracker* and a selected spring gala, both of which feature professional guest artists.
- Corpus Christi Symphony Orchestra: This orchestra has welcomed internationally renowned guest artists like Felipe Entremont, Van Cliburn, and Itzhak Perlman.
- South Texas Institute for the Arts: This art museum is home to traveling exhibits of painting, sculpture, and photography. Its permanent collection of photographs includes works by Ansel Adams and Victoria Livingston.
- The Asian Cultures Museum and Educational Center features Oriental art, sculpture, paintings, scale models of famous pagodas, shrines and temples, and the largest U.S. collection of hand-crafted Hakata dolls.

Those drawn to history will find much to enjoy in the Coastal Bend.

Fulton Mansion State Historical Park and Heritage Park

Fulton Mansion State Historical Park features a completely preserved Victorian mansion built in 1874. This three-story French Second Empire-style home sits on a 2.3-acre lot overlooking Aransas Bay.

Nine historic restored homes preserve the area's diverse heritage in Corpus Christi's Heritage Park. The Galvan House serves as the Multicultural Center, featuring changing art exhibits depicting the city's heritage.

King Ranch

At 825,000 acres, the King Ranch near Kingsville is larger than Rhode Island, and one of the largest ranches in the world. Founded in 1853, the ranch is home to 60,000 cattle. The Santa Gertrudis and King Ranch Santa Cruz breeds were developed here, along with the first registered American Quarter Horse.

Various Sights

The missions of Goliad, 75 miles north of Corpus Christi, preserve the story of the region's role in Texas independence. The Presidio La Bahìa, designated a National Historic Landmark, is considered the world's finest example of a Spanish frontier fort. It is also the most fought-over fort in Texas history, having witnessed six national revolutions and wars for independence.

While you're there, visit Our Lady of Loreto Chapel, the oldest building in the old fort compound. You can also visit the Mission Espíritu Santo, founded in 1749. Other interesting sites include the Market House Museum, designated a State Archaeological Landmark, and the Hanging Tree, an oak tree that between 1846 and 1870 served as the site of court sessions.

General Ignacio Zaragoza

Goliad also is home to the birthplace of General Ignacio Zaragoza. Educated in Mexico, the general joined the Mexican army and worked his way up to general. At the Battle of Pueblo, Mexico, on May 5, 1862, Gen. Zaragoza's forces defeated a French army of intervention. The date—May 5, 1862—became known as *Cinco de Mayo*, a national holiday celebrated in Mexico and much of Texas.

Over the years, Coastal Bend residents have found plenty of other reasons to celebrate. The region's mild weather makes it a perfect spot for festivals. They include:

- Aransas Pass Shrimporee: This annual festival honors Aransas Pass's number-one industry—shrimping. The Shrimporee

Sunsets are only the beginning. Corpus Christi offers visitors great weather, unique attractions and dining, and a spectacular view.

celebrates this tiny creature with a shrimp-eating contest, men's sexy legs contest, parade, children's area, carnival, and the Great Outhouse Race.

- Bayfest: Bayfest provides Corpus Christi and other area residents a variety of entertainment such as carnival rides, fireworks, music, a parade, and food.
- Buccaneer Days and Rodeo: This annual festival celebrates the 1519 discovery of Corpus Christi Bay. Activities include a rodeo, an illuminated night parade, fireworks, music, and carnival.
- Harbor Lights Festival and Boat Parade: The official lighting of the city's 75-foot-tall Christmas tree highlights this annual celebration. Activities include a children's parade, live entertainment, and an illuminated boat parade.
- La Posada de Kingsville: A reenactment of La Posada—the trip Mary and Joseph took as they searched for lodging on Christmas Eve—is a high point for this Christmas celebration. Other events include a downtown lighting ceremony, caroling, and breakfast with Santa Claus.
- Fulton Oysterfest: You'll find oysters by the bucket at this annual celebration honoring the slippery bivalve. An estimated 200,000 oysters are consumed during this three-day salute that includes oyster shucking and oyster eating contests and a carnival.
- Texas Jazz Festival: The longest running free festival in the country features jazz, blues, salsa, and other music in the open-air atmosphere along the Corpus Christi bayfront.

Corpus Christi offers visitors great entertainment when the sun goes down. This flourishing downtown nightlife entertains music lovers of all kinds.

Sports fans find plenty to cheer about in the Coastal Bend. The Corpus Christi Ice Rays, the city's semi-professional hockey team, play each fall and winter at Memorial Coliseum. The Texas A&M University-Corpus Christi men's and women's basketball teams also play there.

Texas A&M University-Kingsville boasts men's teams in baseball, basketball, cross-country, and track, while women compete in volleyball, basketball, softball, cross-country, and track. The Texas A&M University-Kingsville football program is considered one of the best NCAA Division II programs in the nation, and each year several area high school teams are ranked among the Top 10 statewide.

Coastal Bend residents have seized upon one of the area's natural assets—the wind—to attract another popular sporting event. Each year, Corpus Christi hosts the U.S. Open Windsurfing Regatta on Corpus Christi Bay, an event that attracts top windsurfers from throughout the world.

Golf, sailing, boating, windsurfing, kayaking, and personal watercraft are popular here too. Water sports enthusiasts find much to enjoy in the Coastal Bend. Chances are you'll find plenty to enjoy, too, whether it's on the water, at the beach, or inside the many fine attractions, shops, and restaurants throughout the Coastal Bend. ■

Enjoying the wind and waves is easy to do in Corpus Christi, with clears skies, light winds, outstanding beaches, and beautiful waters.

CORPUS CHRISTI

Marina Grand Hotel

Longtime visitors to Corpus Christi know that no matter how much the city changes, they can always count on seeing at least one old friend when they visit. For more than three decades, the 11-story, blue-and-white hotel overlooking beautiful Corpus Christi Bay has welcomed travelers to the Sparkling City By The Sea.

Now known as the Marina Grand Hotel, 300 North Shoreline Blvd., it first opened its doors in 1967, operating for more than 20 years as the full-service, four-star Sheraton Marina Inn. The Spanish Main Restaurant on the 11th floor served as the hub for Corpus Christi's social life, hosting numerous banquets and meetings in its rooftop ballroom. Then, more than ten years ago, the owners sold the property, which was then resold several more times.

Built in 1966 as an 11 story full-service hotel.

The King upgrade room is equipped with a microwave, refrigerator, inroom coffeemaker, and inroom safe. All rooms with balconies overlook the bay.

As the hotel changed hands, it began to lose some of its original luster until Kabir Investment Corporation purchased it in 1997 and updated it to meet the needs of modern business and vacation leisure travelers. The $2 million upgrade covered every aspect of the hotel, from the first-floor lobby to the three-and-a-half-star restaurant on the hotel's top floor.

Lobby improvements made the hotel entrance both more attractive and easier to move around in. New wallpaper, paint, curtains, a floor-to-ceiling glass cylinder, leather wing-backed chairs, and the original marble floors lend an elegant feel to the room.

No trip to the lobby would be complete without stopping to admire a replica of a 17th century Dutch man-of-war ship built by local craftsman Buzz Veazey for the hotel's original owners. The ship has found a new home in front of a mural painted by local artist Guy Morrow, whose works have been displayed at the U.S. embassy in Moscow and who is listed in "Who's Who in American Art." The handmade ship, which took more than two years to build, features authentic Dutch architecture and workable parts, and is trimmed with traditional Dutch lions, cupid dolls, and the Dutch coat-of-arms. The hull is made of western cedar, adorned by carvings of Oriental teak, Honduran mahogany, and African black ebony. The yardarms and mast are made from birch, while the block and tackles are from cherry and Brazilian rosewood.

The GrandView Restaurant on the 11th floor is aptly named, offering visitors a panoramic view of Corpus Christi Bay. It opened on March 9, 1998, following a total renovation to its dining and kitchen facilities. The restaurant, which serves continental cuisine with a southwest flair, received a three-and-a-half-star rating from the North American Food Critics Association.

Guestrooms on floors two through ten received major updates too. The hotel's 172 rooms, which include one 3-bedroom suite and three 1-bedroom suites, received new paint, carpeting, padding, plumbing, beds, and 25-inch, remote-controlled color televisions. Many rooms also received completely new furniture. All rooms come with coffeemakers and safes, while others include microwaves and refrigerators. Even the hallways were updated with new paint, carpeting, padding, and lighting.

Other upgrades include new landscaping and improvements to the private balconies that come with every Marina Grand room. The railings on each balcony have been upgraded and the balconies have been painted white and dove gray to complement the building's sky-blue ends.

Other hotel amenities include an outdoor pool, exercise room, business center, and meeting rooms for as many as 200 people. The first-floor Executive Clipper Conference Room features a 14-seat boardroom, while the Galleon room, also on the first floor, can seat as many as 75 people. For larger groups, the GrandView Ballroom, located on the 11th floor, can seat as many as 200 for banquets, meetings, special lunches, and seminars.

Marina view seen from all guest rooms. Corpus Christi Marina is located at the foot of our building.

The view is the best no matter which room you choose.

Home of the famous Tejano singer Selena Quintinallia. Her memorial overlooks Corpus Christi Bay and Marina.

With a new management team in place, the Marina Grand Hotel is poised to capture its share of the Corpus Christi business market. Its primary focus is the corporate business traveler and small business groups, offering quality service in a warm and friendly atmosphere. The hotel also hopes to attract summer vacation travelers, who flock to the city between the Memorial Day and Labor Day weekends.

The Marina Grand Hotel is within walking distance of several fine restaurants, the Corpus Christi Marina, and the 2-mile-long Corpus Christi Seawall, a popular site for walking, biking, and skating. Several local tourist attractions are located nearby, including the USS Lexington Museum on the Bay, Texas State Aquarium, Corpus Christi Museum of Science and History, and the Corpus Christi Cathedral, one of the most architecturally impressive buildings in the region. The hotel also is a short drive away from Corpus Christi Beach and a 20-minute drive from Padre and Mustang island beaches.

Despite its recent emphasis on remodeling, the Marina Grand Hotel is more than brick and mortar. It's also about people. General Manager Shelly Bram says the hotel's friendly, outgoing staff separates it from other hotels in the area. Santos Alejandro, maintenance technician, Teresa Hernandez, housekeeping, and Alicia Garcia, housekeeping, have been with the hotel since it opened in 1967. And Assistant Manager Robert Morin has spent 15 of his 20 years in the hotel industry at the same hotel where his father, Jimmie Morin, worked for 20 years. Morin, who began his hotel career in 1970, returned to the Marina Grand Hotel in 1997 because he wanted to be involved in returning the hotel to its former glory.

After all, you'd expect nothing less from an old friend. ■

Several Miradores del mar located randomly along Shoreline Boulevard. Many hotel guests enjoy a morning, lunchtime, or evening walk along our wide sidewalks.

Overlooking the bay from the second floor level of the hotel.

Ramada Inn Bayfront

At the Ramada Inn Bayfront, each of the hotel's 80 employees is dedicated to the hotel's philosophy of providing his or her personal best. That means ensuring that each customer is treated with the utmost attention to personal comfort and that each staff member is held to a high standard of customer service. "Each employee is committed to doing their personal best for the guests," said Ralph B. Ehrlich, hotel general manager. "Hospitality is our asset and our trademark."

In upholding its commitment to hospitality, the Ramada Inn Bayfront continues a historic tradition of service that dates back to 1912. It occupies the site that was formerly the Nueces Hotel, built in 1912-1913 and famed throughout the region for its quality accommodations for early travelers. With a banquet hall, two private dining rooms, and 250 guest rooms, the six-story Nueces Hotel was considered the finest hotel in South Texas for its time. It survived the ups and downs of the city's early economy, as well as the devastation wreaked by the 1919 hurricane. For half a century, the Nueces Hotel served as a gracious focus for civic and social activities as well as a pleasant haven for many vacationers. Registered guests included such famous names as politicians Williams Jennings Bryan, General John J. Pershing, and Lyndon Baines Johnson.

But the hotel's longevity came to an end in 1970, when the fury of Hurricane Celia caused such extensive damage that the old hotel was condemned and demolished a year later. On the site, the current 10-story hotel was built as La Quinta Royale. In 1990,

With a major renovation just completed, this hotel sparkles in Corpus Christi.

the Corpus Christi HIMC Limited Partnership acquired the hotel and undertook extensive remodeling. The hotel was renamed the Ramada Inn Bayfront and became part of the Ramada franchise in 1994. Today, the legacy of the old Nueces Hotel is recognized with a plaque from the Texas Historical Commission. But the same amenities that drew early visitors to this locale continue to attract customers to the Ramada Inn Bayfront. The 10-story hotel is located in the central part of downtown, with a scenic view of the Corpus Christi Bayfront. It offers 200 guest rooms, 16,000 square feet of meeting space, an in-house coffee shop called The Palms, a casual lounge called the Sports Pub, and an atrium lounge. The new rooftop LaVista Ballroom provides a panoramic view. There is an exercise room, a second-story rooftop swimming pool, and a gift shop that sells postcards, swimwear, tee-shirts, and more. Located only 15 minutes from Corpus Christi International Airport, the Ramada Inn Bayfront allows vacationers ready access to deep sea fishing, sailing, and windsurfing. From trade shows to football clinics, military reunions to weddings, the Ramada annually hosts numerous conferences and visiting business groups. And with more than 80 employees, the hotel prides itself on a professional conference and catering staff that can assist with any requirement, from personalized menus to board room space. ∎

The atrium lounge features a grand piano.

Pagan-Lewis Motors, Inc.

John S. Pagan and the automobile are a marriage made in heaven, or at least someplace close—Texas.

It all began in the mid-1950s when he became an Edsel dealer in Galveston, Texas, and he continues to this day as the owner of Pagan-Lewis Motors, Inc., a Lincoln-Mercury-Jeep-Subaru dealership at 3737 South Padre Island Drive in Corpus Christi.

Pagan's love of automobiles extends to his Aransas Autoplex in Aransas Pass, a Chevrolet-Buick-Pontiac-GMC-Geo-Oldsmobile dealership, and his Indy Racing League Team, which competes in open-wheel races such as the Indianapolis 500. A second-place finish in 1999 with Jeff Ward behind the wheel shows the positive results of a strong commitment, the same type of commitment of quality service given to customers of Pagan-Lewis Motors.

Through the years, Pagan-Lewis Motors has sold a variety of automobiles, including the Pantera, an imported mid-engine, high-performance spin-off of the Lotus and the DeLorean, a sleek, upscale automobile immortalized in the "Back to The Future" movies.

Pagan bought the Corpus Christi dealership in 1957 along with another man, Ray Lewis, who later decided to pursue other interests. Pagan decided not to change the name, which had already become associated with providing Coastal Bend residents with quality products and services.

Originally located near the Corpus Christi bayfront, Pagan-Lewis Motors now resides along Corpus Christi's busy South Padre Island Drive, the Coastal Bend's retail mecca of car dealerships, malls, and shopping centers.

This convenient location has been good to both Pagan-Lewis Motors and Coastal Bend customers, who choose Pagan-Lewis because of its dedication to providing excellent service beginning with the purchase of a new or used car and continuing throughout the entire life of a selected vehicle.

Pagan-Lewis Motors' 3737 South Padre Island Drive location is easily found on the eastbound frontage road between Carroll Lane and Weber Street. Getting to the dealership is just as easy as purchasing a Lincoln, Mercury, Jeep, or Subaru vehicle at Pagan-Lewis Motors.

Pagan-Lewis offers customers a wide range of automotive services. Its five-acre site features approximately 250 new and 100 used vehicles, a complete service facility, full-service body shop, parts department with $1 million worth of inventory, financing department, leasing department, and rental vehicles available on site.

Their service department performs major and minor repairs on all makes and models of cars, while its body shop can straighten frames, do custom paint work, and perform a thorough cleaning of your automobile. Having a well-stocked parts department allows Pagan-Lewis Motors to provide quicker response time to any ailment your vehicle might have.

Its leasing department can provide short-term or long-term leases from a day to several years, and its financing department stands ready to provide a variety of special financing programs with low rates, extended terms, and life and accident insurance.

Pagan-Lewis Motors can also help you acquire insurance and financing for your purchases and offers extended service policies on most of the vehicles it sells. Its reputation is such that many customers buy their cars over the telephone, selecting a model, negotiating price, and taking possession after a Pagan-Lewis employee delivers it to their homes.

Pagan, who also owns Budget Rent-A-Car at the Corpus Christi International Airport and Accent on Travel, 5433 South Staples Street, plans to keep up his lifelong love affair with the automobile. Which means Coastal Bend customers will continue to benefit from the excellent products and service offered by Pagan-Lewis Motors, Inc. ■

Pagan-Lewis Motors proudly represents Daimler Chrysler Motors. Specializing in the world renowned Jeep brand, Pagan-Lewis offers the best sport utility vehicles in the area. Several million dollars of inventory are available for your convenience and selection.

Christy Estates Suites

Tired of staying in cramped hotel rooms?

Then next time you're planning a trip to Corpus Christi, check into Christy Estates Suites, 3942 Holly Road, where you can stay in a full-sized apartment or a luxurious spa suite at or below hotel-room prices.

Christy Estates offers 190 suites, including 43 spa suites, for corporate and leisure travelers planning to stay a day, a week, or several months. Its corporate suites are the largest in the area, offering the business traveler a home away from home—without having to sign a contract.

Corporate suites range from one-bedroom, one-bath 820-square-foot apartments to two-bedroom, two-bathroom 1,000-square-foot apartments. Each suite comes with a fully equipped kitchen, spacious living room, dining room, direct-dial telephones, voice mail, and a master bedroom with a queen- or king-sized bed.

All suites are furnished with beautiful, modern furnishings and linens, two televisions, 24-hour movies (including HBO), along with news and sports channels. Hotel amenities include daily maid service, clock radios, shampoo, and soaps.

Christy Estates Suites' kitchens are stocked with all cooking and eating utensils, cutlery, a full-size range and refrigerator, dishwasher, garbage disposal, microwave, coffee maker, can opener, toaster, linens, and more.

Every suite has private-line, direct-dial speaker telephones with voice mail. Family and friends can call you directly or you can make local calls from your suite at no extra charge.

Want to pamper yourself even more?

Then try one of 43 European fresh-water spa suites lavishly decorated in various themes. Like the corporate suites, each spa suite comes with a full-sized kitchen, dining area, bedroom, and living room, along with a beautifully designed, fully tiled spa with elegant mirrored walls.

See why Corpus Christi *Caller-Times* readers voted Christy Estates Suites "the most relaxing getaway in town." Many locals enjoy the spas so much they visit two or three times a week. Others choose to celebrate birthdays, anniversaries, and honeymoons there.

Some suites even come with Swedish dry saunas that provide a relaxing and cleansing dry heat bath in a well-insulated room. These luxurious sauna suites feature grade-A western red cedar interiors and glass paneled doors.

Each theme spa suite comes with a 40-inch color television in the living room, remote-controlled television in the bedroom, elegant mirrored walls, special-effect lighting, and a luxurious Italian ebony bath.

Christy Estates Suites offers the luxury of a hotel with the convenience of an apartment complex, including pre-assigned covered parking and two laundry facilities. You'll find more than 6,000 trees and shrubs on the beautifully landscaped grounds, along with two large swimming pools and an outdoor spa.

Christy Estates offers non-smoking suites and accepts all major credit cards. Reduced weekly and monthly rates are available.

Christy Estates is only minutes from golf courses, tennis courts, and fishing facilities, and you'll find museums, historic sites, Padre Island, and the Texas State Aquarium a short drive away.

So the next time you stay in Corpus Christi, whether for business or pleasure, why not treat yourself to a new experience in lodging—spacious, luxurious accommodations at surprisingly low prices. ∎

Photo by Bryan Tumlinson.

CORPUS CHRISTI

Enterprise Index

AEP-Central Power and Light
539 North Carancahua Street
Corpus Christi, Texas 78403
Phone: 361-881-5300
Fax: 361-880-6198
www.aep.com
Pages 96-97

Christy Estates Suites
3942 Holly Road
Corpus Christi, Texas 78415
Phone: 361-854-1091
Fax: 361-854-4766
E-mail: christy@christyestatessuites.com
www.christyestatessuites.com
Page 154

City of Corpus Christi
1201 Leopard Street
Corpus Christi, Texas 78401
PO Box 9277
Corpus Christi, Texas 78469
Phone: 361-880-3220
Fax: 361-880-3839
E-mail: davidg@ci.corpus-christi.tx.us
www.ci.corpus-christi.tx.us
Pages 114-115

Collier, Johnson & Woods, P.C.
555 North Carancahua, Suite 1000
Corpus Christi, Texas 78478-0052
Phone: 361-884-9347
Fax: 361-884-9422
Page 123

Corpus Christi Chamber of Commerce
PO Box 640
Corpus Christi, Texas 78403
Phone: 361-881-1800
Fax: 361-888-5627
E-mail: parredondo@thecchamber.org
www.corpuschristichamber.org
Pages 112-113

Corpus Christi Convention & Visitors Bureau
PO Box 2664
Corpus Christi, Texas 78403
Phone: 800-678-OCEAN
Fax: 361-887-9023
www.corpuschristi-tx-cvb.org
Pages 146-149

Corpus Christi Medical Center
PO Box 8991
Corpus Christi, Texas 78468-8991
Phone: 361-761-1000
Fax: 361-761-1115
www.ccmedicalcenter.com
Page 139

Driscoll Children's Hospital
3533 South Alameda Street
Corpus Christi, Texas 78411
Phone: 361-694-5000
www.driscollchildrens.org
Pages 136-137

DuPont
PO Box JJ
(Highway 361)
Ingleside, Texas 78362
Phone: 361-776-6672
Fax: 361-776-6614
E-mail: phyllis.s.felkner-1@usa.dupont.com
Page 108

Fields, Nemec & Co., P.C.
PO Box 23067
Corpus Christi, Texas 78403
501 South Tancahua Street
Corpus Christi, Texas 78401
Phone: 361-883-7475
Fax: 361-883-2438
E-mail: kdenson@fncpc.com
www.fncpc.com
Page 125

Fulton Construction/Coastcon Corp.
PO Box 9486
Corpus Christi, Texas 78469
Phone: 361-993-5200
Fax: 361-993-8005
Pages 128-129

Haeber Roofing Company
2833 Holly Road
Corpus Christi, Texas 78415
Phone: 361-851-8142
Fax: 361-851-8062
Page 133

Hilb, Rogal and Hamilton Company
5733 South Padre Island Drive
Corpus Christi, Texas 78412
Phone: 361-993-2041
Fax: 361-852-8244
E-mail: dcavenah@hrhcrp.com
www.hrh.com
Page 116

Horton Automatics
4242 Baldwin Boulevard
Corpus Christi, Texas 78405-3399
Phone: 361-888-5591
Fax: 361-887-6821
www.hortondoors.com
Page 106

Hunter & Handel P.C.
555 North Carancahua, Suite 1600, Tower II
Corpus Christi, Texas 78478-0801
Phone: 361-884-8777
Fax: 361-884-1628
E-mail: lawyers@hunterhandel.com
www.hunterhandel.com
Pages 120-121

Marina Grand Hotel
300 North Shoreline Boulevard
Corpus Christi, Texas 78401
Phone: 361-883-5111
Fax: 361-883-7702
E-mail: shellyb@kabircc.com
Pages 150-151

Moorhouse Construction Company
5826 Bear Lane
Corpus Christi, Texas 78405
Phone: 361-883-5993
Fax: 361-883-7417
E-mail: burt@moorhousecc.com
www.moorhousecc.com
Page 130

Naismith Engineering, Inc.
4501 Gollihar
Corpus Christi, Texas 78411
Phone: 361-814-9900
Fax: 361-814-4401
E-mail: khohle@naismith-engineering.com
www.naismith-engineering.com
Page 122

Occidental Chemical Corporation
PO Box CC
Ingleside, Texas 78362
Phone: 361-776-6000
Fax: 361-776-6011
E-mail: pierre_rabalais@oxy.com
Page 107

Pagan-Lewis Motors, Inc.
3737 South Padre Island Drive
Corpus Christi, Texas 78415
Phone: 361-855-8400
Fax: 361-855-2181
E-mail: pagancar@trip.net
www.paganlewismotors.com
Page 153

Port of Corpus Christi
PO Box 1541
Corpus Christi, Texas 78403
Phone: 361-882-5633
Fax: 361-882-7110
www.portofcorpuschristi.com
Pages 98-99

Prudential Real Estate Center
14200 South Padre Island Drive
Corpus Christi, Texas 78418
Phone: 361-949-7033
Fax: 361-949-7235
E-mail: jackypru@ccbor.org
Page 132

Ramada Inn Bayfront
601 North Water Street
Corpus Christi, Texas 78401
Phone: 361-882-8100
Fax: 361-888-6540
E-mail: ramadacc@intcomm.net
www.ramada-cc.com
Page 152

Regional Transportation Authority
5856 Bear Lane
Corpus Christi, Texas 78405
Phone: 361-289-2712
Fax: 361-289-3057
Page 100

Richter Architects
201 South Upper Broadway
Corpus Christi, Texas 78401
Phone: 361-882-1288
Fax: 361-882-1388
E-mail: erichter@richterarchitects.com
www.richterarchitects.com
Page 124

SOL Communications
One Shoreline Plaza
South Tower, 18th Floor
Corpus Christi, Texas 78401
Phone: 361-879-0260
Fax: 361-879-0255
www.solpcs.com
Page 102

Southwestern Bell
406 North Carancahua, Room 100
Corpus Christi, Texas 78401
Phone: 361-881-7115
Fax: 361-881-2253
E-mail: jj1763@txmail.sbc.com
www.swbell.com
Page 103

Surgicare of Corpus Christi
718 Elizabeth Street
Corpus Christi, Texas 78404
Phone: 361-882-3204
Fax: 361-886-6322
Page 138

U.S. Cellular
6047 Weber Road
Corpus Christi, Texas 78415
Phone: 361-946-7000
Fax: 361-946-7002
www.uscellular.com
Page 101

Whataburger, Inc.
PO Box 6220
Corpus Christi, Texas 78466
Phone: 361-878-0650
www.whataburger.com
Pages 142-145

Wilkinson/Reed Development, Inc.
410 South Padre Island Drive, Suite 205
Corpus Christi, Texas 78405
Phone: 361-289-2691
Fax: 361-289-2613
E-mail: wrdevelp@flash.net
Page 131

Patrons:
Coastal Refining & Marketing, Inc.
Gary B. Pearce & Company
Humana Inc.
San Patricio County Economic Development Corporation
Valero Refining Company
Wiley Maden Co.
World Financial Group, Inc.

Bibliography

Centennial History of Corpus Christi. Published by the *Corpus Christi Caller-Times*, 1953.

Corpus Christi Caller-Times newspaper archives. Corpus Christi, Texas.

Corpus Christi Chamber of Commerce, various publications.

Fehrenbach, T.R. *Lone Star: A History of Texas and the Texans*. The Macmillan Company, 1968.

Holt, Harold R. *A Birder's Guide to the Texas Coast*. American Birding Association, Inc., 1993.

Rafferty, Robert R. "Texas Coast and the Rio Grande Valley," *Texas Monthly Guidebooks*. Gulf Publishing Company, 1991.

Webb, Walter Prescott. *The Handbook of Texas*. The Texas State Historical Association, Austin, 1952.

Index

AEP-Central Power and Light, 96-97, 156

agriculture, 34, 68, 77, 90, 114

Aker Gulf Marine Fabricators, Inc., 68

American GI Forum, 9, 19

Amos, Tony, 9

Antonio E. Garcia Arts Education Center, 56

APAC Teleservices, 68

Aransas Pass, 49, 59, 85, 148, 153

Armstrong, Anne and Tobin, 9

Army, 9, 19, 40-41, 43-44, 100, 112, 114, 148

Army Aeronautical Depot Maintenance Center, 43

Art Center of Corpus Christi, 56

Arts and Sciences Park, 25, 56

Asian Cultures Museum and Education Center, 25, 56, 74, 148

Baffin Bay, 85

Ballet Nacional, 57, 147

Balli, Nicolas, 17

Bay Area Medical Center, 48-49, 53, 128

Bayfront Plaza, 57

Bethune Day Care center, 9

Bibbs, Ernestine, 9

Billing Concepts, 68

bird watching, 82-83, 85-86, 146-147

boating, 24, 147, 149

Borghum, Gutzon, 24

Buccaneer Days PRCA Rodeo, 59, 61

Burgee, John, 56

cancer treatment, 48, 51

cardiac care, 48-49

Catholic schools, 75

cattle, 17-19, 57, 68, 86, 90, 137, 148

Center for Bioacoustics, 77

Center for Coastal Studies, 77

Central Flyway, 82

Christus Health, 48-49

Christus Spohn hospitals, 49-50

Christy Estates Suites, 154, 156

CITGO Corpus Christi Refining, 68

Citrus Center, 77

City of Corpus Christi, 17, 25, 41, 66, 74, 111, 114-115, 121, 129, 133, 146, 156

Civil War, 18

climate, 10, 19, 24, 40, 66, 68, 82, 90, 98, 113, 125

Coastal Bend, 10, 42, 100-101, 108, 112, 121-123, 138, 146-149, 153

Coastal Javelina, Inc., 68

Coastal Refining & Marketing, Inc., 122, 156

Cole Park, 25, 59

Collier, Johnson & Woods, P.C., 123, 156

Commander Mine Warfare Group, 42

Commander of Naval Air Training, 42

Corpus Christi Army Depot, 41, 43-44, 100, 112

Corpus Christi Ballet, 57, 148

Corpus Christi Bay, 9-10, 16-17, 19, 24, 27, 40-43, 48-49, 51, 56, 59, 66, 68, 74, 77, 82, 86, 90, 99, 101, 103, 129, 132, 139, 143-144, 146, 149-151

Corpus Christi Beach, 25, 40, 100, 147, 151

Corpus Christi Cancer Center, 51

Corpus Christi Cathedral, 59, 148, 151

Corpus Christi Chamber Music Society, 59

Corpus Christi Chamber of Commerce, 66, 111-113, 121, 129, 156

Corpus Christi Community Concert Series, 59

Corpus Christi Concert Ballet, 57, 148

Corpus Christi Convention & Visitors Bureau, 66, 141, 146, 156

Corpus Christi Greyhound Race Track, 19, 27, 128

Corpus Christi Independent School District, 74, 133

Corpus Christi Lab, 49

Corpus Christi Literary Reading Series, 59

Corpus Christi Medical Center, 49, 135, 139, 156

Corpus Christi Museum of Science and History, 25, 74, 115, 147, 151

Corpus Christi Naval Hospital, 49

Corpus Christi Regional Economic Development Corporation, 66

Corpus Christi Ship Channel Company, 19

Corpus Christi Symphony, 58, 74, 148

Corpus Christi Warm Springs Rehabilitation Hospital, 50

cost of living, 66, 68

crops, 68, 107

Davis, Jefferson, 17

de Pineda, Alonso Alvarez, 17

de Vaca, Alvar Nunez Cabeza, 17

Deep Sea Roundup, 59

Del Mar College, 56, 74-75, 112, 124

Distinguished Visitors in the Arts Series, 59

Doctors Regional Medical Center, 49

Driscoll Children's Hospital, 49-51, 135-137, 156

Driscoll Children's Rehabilitation Center, 50

Driscoll, Clara, 49, 136

Driscoll, Julia, 49, 136

Driscoll, Robert, 49, 136

Driscoll, Robert Jr., 49, 136

DuPont, 108, 156

East West Powerboat Shootout, 59
education, 72-79
E.I. DuPont de Nemours & Co., 68
employment, 66, 75, 108, 121

farming, 19, 71, 125
Fields, Nemec & Co., P.C., 125, 156
First Data Corp., 68
First United Methodist Church, 59
fishing, 21, 24-26, 82, 85, 90, 146-147, 152, 154
Frederic Chopin Society, 59
Frissell, Toni, 56
Fulton Construction/Coastcon Corp., 128-129, 156
Fulton Oysterfest, 59, 149
Futuremarket Telecenter, Inc., 68

Garcia, Dr. Hector P., 9, 19, 76
Grant, Ulysses S., 17
Great Texas Coastal Birding Trail, 82, 146
Greater Kingsville Economic Development Council, 9
Gulf King Seafood Co., 68

Haeber Roofing Company, 133, 156
Halo-Flight Inc., 51
Harbor Island, 85, 99
Harbor Lights Festival and Boat Parade, 59, 149
health care, 19, 48-49, 90, 114, 129, 135-136
Heart Hospital of South Texas, 49
HEB grocery chain, 68
Helicopter Mine Countermeasures Squadron 15, 42
Heritage Park, 25, 148
Hilb, Rogal and Hamilton Company, 116, 156
Hoechst Celanese Technical Center, 68
Horizon Specialty Hospital, 50
Horton Automatics, 68, 105-106, 156
Houston, 24, 35, 48-49, 98, 121, 130, 144
Hunter & Handel P.C., 120-121, 156

Ice Rays, 59-60, 149
Inner Harbor Meeting & Banquet Center, 35
International Resistive Corp. Advanced Film Division, 68

J.F.K. Causeway, 83
job training, 66
John E. Conner Museum, 57, 147
Johnson, Philip, 56
Jones, Luther, 9
Junior League of Corpus Christi, 74, 101

Karankawa Indians, 16-17
KEDT, 74
King Ranch, 18, 56-57, 68, 86, 147-148
King Ranch Museum, 56, 147
King, Richard, 18, 74, 86
Kinney, Henry Lawrence, 17, 112, 114
Kinney's Ranch, 17, 114
Kinney's Trading Post, 40, 114
Koch Refining Co., 68

Lafitte, Jean, 17
Latin America, 56, 66
League of United Latin American Citizens, 19
Lee, Robert E., 17
Legorreta, Ricardo, 56
Lexington Museum on the Bay, 19, 23, 25, 28, 74, 151

Malaquite Beach, 83
manufacturing, 19, 66, 68, 102, 105-108, 112, 123, 125, 128
Marina Grand Hotel, 150-151
Marine Corps, 43-44
Memorial Coliseum, 59-60, 122, 149
Men's Pro Beach Volleyball Competition, 59
Messbarger, Dick, 9
Mexican-American War, 40
military, 9, 19, 35, 38-45, 49, 66, 99, 112, 114, 152
Millward Brown, 68
Moorhouse Construction Company, 130, 156
Moroles, Jesus Bautista, 9
Mustang Island, 85, 112, 124, 151

Naismith Engineering, Inc., 122, 156
National Spill Control School, 77
natural gas, 19, 96
Naval Air Station Corpus Christi, 40-44, 49, 112
Naval Air Station Kingsville, 9, 39, 41, 43
Naval Hospital, 42, 49
Naval Station Ingleside, 41-44, 112, 133
Navy, 18-19, 26, 40-44, 112, 147
Navy's Mine Warfare Center of Excellence, 43
North Bay Hospital, 49
Northwest Regional Hospital, 49

Occidental Chemical Corporation, 68, 156
Ocean Drive, 10, 25, 59
oil, 16, 18-19, 34, 66, 68-69, 90, 112, 125, 147

Padre Island National Seashore, 83-84, 112, 146-147

Pagan-Lewis Motors, Inc., 153, 156
parochial schools, 75
Pearl Harbor, 26, 40-41
petrochemical industry, 19, 35, 66, 68, 98
Port Aransas, 9-10, 26, 59, 85, 146-147
Port of Corpus Christi, 32-37, 66, 95, 98-99, 107, 112, 115, 124, 129, 156
private schools, 75
Prudential Real Estate Center, 132, 156

Ragland Mercantile Building, 57
railroads, 18, 98-99
Ramada Inn Bayfront, 152, 156
ranching, 17-19, 57, 59, 68, 71, 82, 86, 90
Regional Transportation Authority, 9, 95, 100, 131, 133, 156
Richard King High School Planetarium, 74
Richter Architects, 124, 156
Richter, David and Elizabeth Chu, 9
Rincon de Santa Gertrudis Mexican Land Grant, 86
Rio Grande Valley, 40, 77, 98, 133
Roosevelt, Franklin Delano, 85

Sam Kane Beef Processors, 68
Santa Gertrudis Creek, 86
Santa Gertrudis Ranch, 18
schools, 18, 72-79, 97, 100, 103, 107, 130
Selena Auditorium, 57
Selena, 9, 24, 56-57, 59, 146, 151
shipping, 17-18, 32-37, 99, 114
Shoreline Boulevard, 24, 59, 113, 151, 156
Shrimporee, 59
Sisters of Charity of the Incarnate Word, 48-49
SITEL, 68
SOL Communications, 102, 156
South Texas Institute for the Arts, 25, 56, 74, 122, 128-129, 148
South Texas Public Broadcasting System, Inc., 74
South Texas Ranching Heritage Festival, 59
Southwestern Bell, 103, 156
Spohn Health System, 48-49
Surgicare of Corpus Christi, 49, 135, 138, 156

Taylor, Zachary, 17, 40, 114
Texas A&M University-Corpus Christi, 9, 19, 56, 73, 76, 112, 122, 149
Texas A&M University-Kingsville, 56-57, 59, 77-78, 112, 149
Texas A&M University system, 19
Texas Jazz Festival, 59, 149

Texas State Aquarium, 19, 25, 28-29, 74, 112, 123, 128, 146-147, 151, 154
tourism, 19, 22-31, 66, 85, 90, 99-100, 114, 141
Training Air Wing Four, 42

Ullberg, Kent, 59
University of Kingsville, 43
University of Texas Marine Science Institute, 9, 147
U.S. Cellular, 101, 156
USS *Inchon*, 44
USS *Lexington*, 23, 25, 28, 42-43, 146-147, 151
USS *Wisconsin*, 43

Valero Refining Co., 68

Watergarden, 25
Welder Wildlife Foundation's Refuge, 83
Wells Fargo Bank, 68
Whataburger, Inc., 68, 156
wildlife, 83, 85-86, 146-147
Wilkinson/Reed Development, Inc., 131, 156
Wilhelmi, William, 59

Young Audiences programs, 74

Zion, Robert, 25